Chapter 1.

School Project

Jeff McGowan left his school books on the kitchen counter, set the oven and removed the defrosting roast from the fridge. He scrubbed and peeled his potatoes putting them in a sauce pan, covered it and set the spuds on the stove for boiling when his mother got home.

Jeff went to the cupboard, selected green beans and stewed tomatoes and placed them by the sink with the can opener. By this time, the oven was hot. He checked the temperature, placed the beef in a roaster and slid it in.

Judging yesterday's cloth to be serviceable still, he shook it out the sliding glass door and spread it on the dining room table, returned to the kitchen first for plates, then for silver and napkins and set three places. He checked the table, took a look around the kitchen, then located the potato-masher, laying that on the draining board near the cans. Adding some water to the roast and re-covering it, he opened the fridge, took out horseradish, catsup and a can of cherry soda. The condiments he placed on the dining room table along with salt and pepper, made a final pass through the kitchen to collect his books and his pop, and headed upstairs to his room.

Jeff was done with his math in about fifteen minutes, even showing all his work in his unusually meticulous penmanship. History would take longer, but that was a thing to be savored. Yesterday they had started the unit on the later Middle Ages in Tiegs Adams' Your World and Mine. He settled down to read the story at the beginning of the chapter.

He interrupted his reading long enough to go back to his door and yell a greeting downstairs to his Mom who'd now be putting the potatoes on to boil.

"Good evening dear," she called back, amidst cooking noises.

Soon the voice of Lorna, newly arrived from the library, was also wafting excitedly from below.

Everybody was all excited right now about this Community Service Month thing that the Junior and Senior high schools participated in, which ran all through March and was always ended by a big presentation ceremony downtown. This year, as a seventh-grader, Jeff would have his first opportunity to participate, but so far, frankly, everything Jeff'd heard made the whole thing sound like one terrible bore. School activities always put him so much in mind of soccer teams or baseball-and all that implied.

While he read, part of Jeff's mind registered the sounds of Lorna ascending the stairs, rummaging around in her room, then clattering back down again. She must be bugging her friends about some new scheme or other. This unexpected opportunity inspired him to do something he seldom attempted with others home.

With an ear tuned for noises downstairs Jeff slipped secret agent fashion into his sister's room. The door stood ajar and he opened it just wide enough to get through. Jeff stepped carefully, avoiding that floorboard which always squeaked! At the dresser now, he worked at first one end of the drawer, then the other. It slid open without any noise, wide enough for inspection.

Jeff made his selections quickly, rejecting both the faded cotton panties from last year and the elaborately embroidered bikinis, which might be missed. He chose somewhat worn blue pair, with little pink and yellow flowers along the borders. He considered a training bra, but the fear of it's detection under his shirt detoured him. Lorna hardly wore a slip though, and he could take that with impunity.

He slid the top drawer closed and eased open the bottom one, where the orange skirt, seemingly forgotten by his sister resided. He took the skirt then crossed to the closet, moved Lorna's dresses aside and reached the rose-colored slip off of it's hanger. He replaced the dresses, brushing them a little so they'd look undisturbed. Clutching skirt, slip, and panties he made his withdrawal. He calipered the door to it's previous degree of openness then crossed into the bathroom.

Jeff undressed quickly, leaving on his socks, recklessly flinging shorts and undershirt into the hamper. He stepped into the borrowed nylon panties, then worked the slip over his head. Zipping the skirt on the left, Jeff re-donned shoes and shirt, letting the latter hang loosely on the outside, then raised the toilet seat fuzzy toilet seat and sat down.

It took a while to relax to the task, but eventually he peed, reached for paper, rose, replaced panties and flushed, waiting until the tank refilled entirely in order to monitor any approach. Hearing nothing from downstairs he strode as leisurely as he dared down the hall to his own room. Jeff closed the door, settled himself at his desk and read three entire pages in his World History book before he got up again, walked slowly, deliberately across his room, turned and walked back. Reluctantly, he stepped out of the skirt, tucking the slip between his legs, back and front, then pulled on his pants over his sneakers. He was *just safe* when his mother called.

"Je-eff, din-ner!"

Jeff and his Terrible Secret made their way downstairs to sit at the dining room table with his mom and 9th-grade sister.

"So," Mrs. McGowan said, passing around the mashed potatoes. "How is Community Service Month coming along?"

As usual, Lorna was off to the races. "The same old stuff so far," she said, forking fresh-cut green beans through her disapproval. "Most of the girls are doing volunteer work in the nursing home, or stocking shelves at the library. Some of them are even babysitting. A few of the kids are doing some work in the park or yard stuff for the elderly. Nothing of much consequence." Lorna paused for dramatic effect. "If they would have agreed to build that solar pool heater I designed from the black PVC pipes-we really could have made a contribution!"

"Chug-chug-chug-chug-woo-wooooo!" Jeff chimed in, referring to Lorna's oft-stated determination to be an engineer.

"That's enough out of you." His mother worked hard at concealing a smile. "By the way Jeff, how are things going for you Seventh Graders?"

"Not going at all, yet." Jeff shrugged airily. "Besides, you know the big kids'll hog all the good jobs. By the time we get to pick anything there won't be anything to pick."

"That statement hardly makes any sense mathematically Jeff," his sister reprimanded, "but can't you propose something? A project of your own I mean?"

"Don't know." Jeff replied without the world-shaking concern that his sister seemed to bring to just about everything. "Tomorrow'll be the first time we even get to talk about it."

"On the bulletin board are the remaining assignment opportunities for our Community Service Month. We will come to the front of the room in groups of five. When you find a job in which you are interested, you will note the number in the bottom right-hand corner of the job card, and enter that number on the sign-up sheet. Yes, Willard?"

"They aren't cards," said Willy Jackson. "They're pieces of paper."

"Any further disturbance, Willard, and *your* assignment will be after school blackboard monitor-permanently." Ms. Larson pulled a severe face, making as if to enter this on her sign-up sheet.

Willy was in Jeff's group which was the last to go up. The teacher's attention being elsewhere at the moment, Willy popped an ancient wad of bubble gum into his mouth, and blew an enormous bubble. He was virtuously ignored by the three girls in the group, who were studying the offerings left after grades night and eight had made their pick. Jeff decided that Lorna had been right and there really wasn't anything of earth-rocking significance.

"A library job," Jennifer Wright said, a little bit hopefully. "I helped in the school library last year..."

"With Old Lady Pemberton!" Susan Manchester looked pained. "I couldn't handle that."

Willy stretched his gum into a thin, pink ribbon, making as if to coil it in Susan's hair.

"Willard!" Ms. Larson pointed meaningfully at the waste basket.

The absence of the other boy allowed Jeff an opportunity to study one of the less official-looking items on the board. On a sheet of white notebook paper was hand-printed in large letters

> *Blind woman wishes student assistant for*
> *Reading, Light errands, Companionship.*

After that appeared *(girl preferred.)* then a name, address and phone number.

"I wonder what kind of stuff this person wants to read," Jeff mused aloud.

"Oh," Susan looked. "Julie Gardener tried working with that blind woman last year. Julie said that she was some kind of a pain!"

"Well," Jennifer temporized, "they might just have gotten off on the wrong foot. You read so well Jeffrey, and you're so helpful- I'd try it if I were you."

"'**I'd try it if I were you.**'" Willy shoved Jeff aside to stare at the note. "You'd be perfect for the job, McGowan. You're such a **woman!**"

Without making a selection, Jeff returned to his desk.

During lunch, he snuck back to his roll-room.

"Oh, Jeff." Surprised, Ms. Larson looked up from her grading. "I've been worried."

"Really?"

"Why, yes. I thought to find your name on several selections, you are always so much the helper and so involved." Forlornly, she studied the depopulated patchwork remaining on the bulletin board.

"Well, there was one job I thought about, but I didn't know if I should."

His teacher stepped up beside him to study the item. "Seems like a natural for you Jeff. Why didn't you sign up?"

Jeff pointed to the pertinent line.

"Oh-well, I can see that you might have doubts, but I imagine this woman simply thought a girl would be a more likely companion, or that a boy your age wouldn't be interested. I think, though, that she underestimates the caliber of our seventh-graders." Playfully, she elbowed Jeff in the ribs. "I know, by the way, who really made the cookies for the P. T. S. A. mid-winter bazaar-your mother let the cat out. Yes. I think this Irene Carrol person could learn a thing or two from somebody like you."

Jeff didn't know whether to feel complimented or just embarrassed, which he already was. "You think I should try for the job then?"

"Why not? Nobody else has, and the most she can do is say no." Ms. Larson detached the piece of paper from the board, presenting it to Jeff. "Or would you like me to talk to her?" she offered.

"No. Thanks. I guess I'll do it myself. The most she can do is say no."

"Great attitude! You must have wise teachers." She patted Jeff on the arm. "Is this why Willy was giving you a hard time this morning?"

"I guess."

She sighed.

When the bulk of students had gone home or reported for team sports, Jeff took his third drink of water and headed slowly for the pay phone on the second-floor landing. The phone rang twice, three times-(Nobody's home. I'll try another time.)

"Hello?"

"Hello…." Jeff's nervousness caused his voice to climb even beyond it's accustomed treble pitch. "I-I'm calling from the junior high?"

"Oh, yes." The woman's voice sounded happy-even excited. "You're one of the girls who volunteers."

"Yes," Jeff said. She hadn't even made it a question.

"That's wonderful! Would you like to come over?"

Jeff's thoughts raced. *Always sleep on a big decision*, his family's matriarchal wisdom has instructed. "Would tomorrow be alright?" He looked at the piece of paper. "I can get there by three-thirty."

"Of course. You know where I am then?"

Jeff recited the street name and number.

"Third house on the right going north. Real messy front yard." She giggled. "What's your name, by the way?"

"J-Jennifer…" Jeff said.

"Mine's Irene. I suppose you knew that. Great to meet you, Jen. See you tomorrow. We'll have fun!"

Jeff stood there for fully ten minutes contemplating the enormity of what he had just done. Then, seeing the custodian approaching along the hall, he slipped downstairs, avoiding the man's gaze. He walked home along the back streets, through the crisp, clear afternoon, relishing the quiet of the now nearly vacated sidewalks and the lack of need to talk to anybody for the present.

That evening Mrs. McGowan looked up from her plate to note a far-away look on her son's face. "There isn't anything wrong, is there, Jeff?"

"No," he said, perhaps a bit too abruptly.

"Any luck with your projects?"

"Nothing so far…" Lorna answered, glowering at her meal.

"You, Jeff?" their mother persisted.

"Um." Jeff nearly swallowed a bit of chicken the wrong way. "I might have something, maybe…"

"That's nice." Mrs McGowan smiled. "Do you want to tell us about it?"

"I might go read for a blind lady."

Both his mother and Lorna looked slightly surprised.

"Really?" Mrs. McGowan said. "I guess I wouldn't have thought of that as something that would interest you, but, the main thing is to find something worthwhile, then do the very best you can-" Having delivered herself of this sound advice, she returned to her own worries at work. With Tax-time upon herself and everyone else in the accounting office, Heaven knew there was plenty about which to worry…!

After dinner, pleading a need for fresh air, Jeff took the now pocket-worn piece of paper and set out to locate that big-print address. As he walked, a rough plan was forming, whose outcome (whatever it's eventual form) must depend upon timing and the precise lay of the land. Turning up the street he noted shrubbery, foliage, any sort of cover. "Messy yard is right," Jeff said half-aloud as he approached the third house. He stood for a couple of minutes, straining through the darkness at the weather-beaten front door with it's ripped screen, wishing it would open to give him a look at the blind woman, but it did not.

Jeff circled the block once then headed for home again, forcing himself to a trot to counter the wind's increasing chill. He heard Lorna talking on the kitchen phone as he came in. Sounds from his mother's study, off the hall, hinted that she'd brought work home again. Glad enough of the solitude, he tiptoed upstairs.

Chapter 2.

The House With the Lamp Unplugged

Jeff slapped his alarm clock to silence. It has awakened him a half hour earlier than usual. Lorna, who'd got early band practice, is just making her way out the door and Mom has already left for work. Usually, he'd just wolf breakfast and be off to school, but this morning will be different. Jeff has slept in one of Lorna's nightgowns, fancying that any dream he might have would tell him whether or not the thing he contemplates doing is right. He can't remember dreaming though, and his gown wrapped around his legs during the night, waking him up several times. Still, he's thought of little else since yesterday afternoon.

Jeff folded the nightgown so his pillow would hide it, then hurriedly made his bed. He padded down the hall, to the bathroom in just the panties he'd had on underneath. Jeff flushed the toiled before sitting down as he'd seen his mother do.

He stared back at the quizzical face looking at him from the mirror, washed his face, brushed his teeth, then walked into Lorna's room.

Jeff opened the closet, taking down the deep, blue dress from the farthest end and laid the dress, with it's hanger, on the bed. He took a pair of white anklets from her dresser and one of the little sleeveless undershirts he knew girls who didn't yet have bras wore sometimes.

Lorna's shoes were a bit narrow, but in the back of their mother's closet were a pair of brown sandals which Jeff knew to be a very adequate fit. Carrying the dress and other things, Jeff hurried along to his room, securing the sandals and also taking from a little top drawer in Mom's bureau, a scarf with blue and yellow flowers on a white background.

Sitting now on the edge of his bed, Jeff pulled on the undershirt, put on first the anklets then his own blue-topped crew socks, then got quickly into his school clothes. He went and took a paper sack from the kitchen cupboard, writing "Gym clothes, McGowan" on the sack, then ran back up to his room. He folded the dress as well as he could, placed the sandals first in the sack, then added the dress and scarf. He ate his breakfast with the sack in front of him on the kitchen table. Then, with it and the two school books under his arm, set off down the street toward the junior high.

School activities this day rather swirled and eddied about Jeff McGowan with scant notice from him. *Do I dare?* He demanded of himself a few dozen times during his periods until classes ended. *Do I really dare--?* He managed to avoid Willy Jackson to his not inconsiderable relief, but he ended standing behind Jennifer Wright in the hot lunch line during seventh-grade break. He nearly stepped aside to keep from being noticed. As luck would have it, Susan was not with her (for once), and she turned around, smiling at him.

"Hello, Jeffrey. Did you call her?"

Jeff nodded, feeling his ears redden uncomfortably.

"Yes?" Jennifer prompted. "And what did she say?"

"We're going to talk," Jeff told her.

"Oh, wonderful!" she enthused. "It'll be just fine. I'm certain that she'll be happy to work with a nice person like you."

Jennifer glanced hastily around her then leaned close. "Susan still hasn't found anything," she confided. "I ran over to the library right after school and put my name down."

"That's great." Jeff returned her kind wishes. He filled his tray with burger, tater-tots, jello cubes and apple wedges and made for a relatively unoccupied corner of the cafeteria.

Sixth period was Language Arts, which usually held Jeff's attention, but today he contributed little, not even offering any calculatedly discordant verbs, nouns, or adjectives for the monster Mad-lib Miss Bulletin allowed "since class is so quiet today." Jeff was first out of class at the bell and down to his locker to get the clandestine gym bag.

At first, changing seemed an insuperable difficulty. But, reconnoitering the neighborhood the afternoon previous, Jeff had noticed a dense clump of bushes within easy dash from Irene's house. So, he was out of the building ahead of the pack, putting enough distance between himself and school to minimize the danger of unwanted companionship. Clutching his sack, he made quickly for the correct block, then watched to make sure no-one was in the immediate vicinity, nor would be for a few minutes.

The block was relatively secluded. The yard was indeed a jumble of last summer's weeds and somebody else's garbage-unless she used old tires for something, Jeff reflected, and breaks beer bottles just for fun. The house itself was a weathered green-gray with dirty green trim. The screen door had a big hole in it. A rusty garbage can lay on it's side, the lid a few feet away. Jeff slipped into the hiding place he'd marked for his transition to Jennifer.

Jeff knelt in the matted grass carpet under the bushes, working quickly to avoid needlessly dampening his pants-legs. Carefully, he removed his shirt, stuffing it into the bag before extracting the dress which he worked down over his head.

Squatting now, resting first on one foot and then the other, he took off one shoe then a pant-leg, slipping a sandal on the foot, remembered his double sock, slid the sandal off again, removed the outer sock, replaced the sandal. The process was repeated, a little more successfully this time, for the other leg and foot. He removed the scarf from the bag before including his shoes, at the bottom so as not to soil his other clothes. He continued squatting, careful not to drag the skirt on the ground while folding the scarf diagonally as he'd seen his Mom and sister do, then laid the long fold across his forehead, concealing rather more of his face than he might have. He tied the scarf under his chin, wishing he'd brought a compact or something so Jennifer could see herself. "She" slid the dress as well into place, as was manageable in this cramped position, peered out of the bushes in all possible directions, then taking a long and somewhat painful breath, bounded clear of the bushes, straightening the dress, catching up bag and coat.

When confronted by the imminent meeting, now so close, the strong urge was to turn and run or slink back into the bushes. No. Neither course was possible- and standing undecided, out here in plain view, was riskier still.

For no other reason just now than to gain the safety of a house, Jeff/Jennifer moved as quickly as was possible on the unfamiliar shoes, toward the porch and up the steps. (Oh God, what if she's not home?)

"Oh, Jenny!" The chain was removed from the door and it swung inward. The woman fumbled at the screen door, and her visitor stepped aside in order to allow it to swing outward. "Come in," Irene called over her shoulder as she turned back into the living room, in order to regain the knob of the wooden inner door.

The living room was dimly lit. Instinctively Jeff moved to the end-table where a lamp stood. The switch clicked one, then again, with no result.

Irene heard the sound, evidently. "Oh, I'm sorry," she said. "The bulb must be burned out. Come into the kitchen. We'll sit in there. The light's good-I think." She closed the door and with one hand slightly ahead of her, made her way across the not-too-clean carpet into the kitchen. The overhead light was cobwebby, but functional.

Jeff/Jennifer pulled out one of the cracked, cane-backed kitchen chairs and sat down gingerly. *Keep your knees together. You've got a dress on.* At the moment, "she" felt very, very foolish.

"Tell me about yourself," Irene was saying. "I'm Irene, but you know that already. I'm real glad you could make it. Would you like a can of diet Pepsi?"

"Yes. That would be nice." *Does my voice really sound like a girl?* "Please."

Irene went to the refrigerator, took out two cans of pop, turned back to the table, thumping it energetically. "Oh," she said in seeming response to her guest's look of consternation. "I'm just checking to see if I've left anything standing on the table. Sometimes I forget."

The table held. Jennifer noticed as if by afterthought some closed books and some loose sheets of cream-colored paper, one of which fluttered to the floor as Irene banged.

"Damned algebra!" She retrieved the paper by moving her hand in widening circles across the linoleum, putting it back with the rest of the mess on the kitchen table. She went to a cupboard and took down a package of Oreos. "I can give you a glass if you want to dunk," she said, "or you can drink it out of the can."

She pushed the pressboard-packed math book aside, sliding the papers beneath the cover. "I just can't seem to get this stuff!" Irene said, slapping the offending volume. She launched then into a lengthy dissertation on the topic.

"I'm sorry," Irene said when they well down their Pepsis. "I started out to ask you about yourself, what kinds of things you like to do- and here I've been jabbering away for the past fifteen minutes, about my own problems. Your turn."

"Not very much to tell, I guess, Jennifer answered, on the verge of defensiveness.

"Horse-puckey!" Irene slurped at her soda. "You offered to come over here and aren't trying to lead me around my own house! That tells me a lot right there."

It was dark by the time Jeff left Irene's house. Passing through the living room it was evident that the lamp wasn't even plugged in. Not very many sighted people visited here. Perhaps Jeff should find more friends for her. But, that might be difficult since Irene thought he was Jennifer. Besides, it was nice to have a special friend of your own-for now, anyway.

After saying good-bye, Jeff had slipped back behind Irene's house and in the shelter of the dilapidated board fence had gotten out of the dress and sandals, resuming his school clothes.

"So, how did your visit go today, Jeff' They were again at the table. Mom had not yet mentioned the fact that he was late for dinner.

"Fine." Jeff thought that something of interest might be required, so he said, almost in clarification "she sews and everything. And-" he looked meaningfully at his sister, "she's interested in algebra!"

"You think this will be an interesting project for school then?" Mrs. McGowan pressed the point with all of the concern of a mother who honestly never quite finds the time to be as much involved in her children's school activities as she'd like to be.

"I think so. At first she wanted-" Jeff broke off.

"Wanted what?" his mother prompted.

"Wanted somebody who was good with a sewing machine," Jeff temporized a little nervously.

"Well," his mother soothed, "it doesn't ever hurt to learn new things."

"That's what I've been trying to tell those lame brains in my class!" Lorna was full of righteous indignation. "If we keep on doing everything the same way they've always been done, we might as well call this 'Odd Jobs Month.'" Lorna considered a moment, then asked "how does she thread a needle, Jeff?"

"She who? You mean Irene?"

"What other She have we been talking about since dinner started?" his sister said in exasperation. *Wouldn't you be astonished?* Jeff couldn't prevent a tiny smirk. "With a little wire loop," he said. "She sticks it through the needle eye, then puts the thread through the loop and the thread comes along with it."

"That makes sense," Lorna allowed.

"What have you found for your own project, Lorna?" Their mother turned slightly away, as if dodging the flood of frustration that seemed imminent.

"Well," Lorna wrinkled her forehead. "Since I probably won't get to do anything that I want to, I think I'll try and find something with the library. I don't know what yet, but at least I'll get to be around books."

"That sounds sensible," Mrs. McGowan agreed.

Daydreaming, Jeff mused about the hole in Irene's screen and the other ideas which had come from their conversation that afternoon.

On his way to his room after dinner, Jeff passed Lorna's open door. His sister sat over a miscellany of balsa wood sheets, exacto knives and glue bottles, evidently assembling a model of some sort. He stood for a moment in the doorway, silently watching her. Lorna drew a razor sharp blade precisely along a pencilled line on the soft wood, laying aside the excised rectangle, then looked up.

"Want something?" she asked.

Jeff nearly went in to seat himself on Lorna's bed as he did sometimes to confide the enormity of the day that had just transpired, but knew of no way to even start. Besides, he was still wearing Lorna's socks and underwear and that would be-well, just too weird. "No," he said. "Not really. I was just watching." He tip-toed away, leaving her to her contrivance.

Jeff had mis-stated the truth when telling his sister of the blind woman's interest in algebra.

"I just can't seem to get it!" Irene had exclaimed, close to tears. "I've got to pass this correspondence course before they'll let me into the college, and this book just won't make sense!" Again she smote the odious text, a plastic-bound book whose pages, Jeff noticed, were also formed in plastic, instead of being punched in paper like the card they'd seen during vision awareness week.

"Can you show me a problem?" he asked. Lorna had drilled him in math rather beyond his seventh-grade requirements.

"Well, here's one." Irene seemingly chose at random from one of the dotted pages. "$3x+2=17$. That doesn't make any sense to me. What the hell's an X?"

"Depends," said Jeff. "Let me show you what my sister taught me." He began to put his hand in his pocket in search of change, remembered suddenly that he had no pockets. "I've got my gym clothes in this sack," Jeff offered lamely. Hoping that she really could not see, Jennifer explored the pockets of Jeff's pants pockets. *I wonder if I should get a purse.* There were three nickels and some pennies. With Irene's help, more pennies were produced and two saucers and a pair of silver kitchen knives.

"These knives are the equal-sign," Jennifer told her, positioning the saucers and utensils in a left to right orientation with respect to Irene. "The plate on your left has three nickels and two pennies on it. That is for 3x+2. The plate on the right has seventeen pennies. Now all we need to remember is that whatever we do to one plate, we have to do to the other. Now, we take two pennies away from each plate and that gives us 3x=15. Now all we have to do is build up the pennies left over into three piles and when they are equal, then each stack is what an x is."

Irene frowned, counting the pennies on the right plate, three by three and building a set of neat little stacks. "Three stacks. Three nickels, Xs I mean," she corrected herself. "That means that every X is equal to 5!"

"That's right."

"What if you've got something like," she perused her plastic math book, "2x+5 = x+8?"

"Now," Jeff moved coins around once more. "You've got two nickels or Xs on the left plate, along with five pennies, and over here on your right, X plus eight."

Carefully, Irene felt both plates, counting coins. "Okay," she said.

"Okay. Now, we'd like, somehow, to get just Xs on one plate, and ones, or regular numbers I mean, on the other. We do that by taking away coins, the same kind and number from each plate."

Irene explored the plates. Tentatively she slid a nickel off each plate. "I've got x+5 = 8," she said hesitantly. "What if I take away five pennies from each side?" She thought another moment. "That leaves, three pennies equals a nickel! You'll never make it in the business world, girl! No. An X equals three? Could that be right?"

"Let's check it," Jeff said, realizing that Irene could not see the grin on her new friend's face.

"What if you have negative numbers?" Irene wanted to know.

"You use more kinds of coins. Maybe dimes for negative ones and quarters for negative Xs."

"I'd always heard that money talks," Irene laughed, "but I never knew it could do algebra."

"My sister is so wonderful!" Jennifer was thoroughly enjoying herself now. "Once she taught me this system for doing my math, I can always hold out on doing my homework till Mom gives me my allowance!" Both girls dissolved into storms of giggles.

It was somewhere near the time that they took reluctant leave of one another, and Jeff re-entered his guise as a young adolescent boy, that Irene said suddenly "Can you get ahold of any Mad magazines?"

"Mad magazines?" Jennifer was unsure that s/he had heard correctly.

"Sure, a Mad," Irene affirmed. "One of the partially sighted girls I used to go to school with would bring her big brother's Mad magazines from home and read them to me. We'd laugh like idiots! Did get in quite a lot of trouble, as I recall, when a teacher's aide caught us in study hall… maybe I shouldn't be trying to corrupt you like that.' A cloud passed momentarily over Irene's face. "I don't know…"

Her friend said, "I might know somebody."

Chapter 3.

"If you help me I'll…"

So, here Jeff was, the next morning before school, waiting by Willie's locker. "Willie…" Jeff called, no louder than was necessary to attract the other's attention.

"Whatcha want, Jeff-ree?" He pronounced the name in a soprano parody.

"Have you got a Mad?"

"Maybe. Who's asking?"

"Well," Jeff hazarded, "a friend of mine wants to see one."

"Why doesn't this friend just get his ass out and buy one?"

"The friend is blind." Jeff said it without thinking, regretting the admission a moment later. "I don't think the grocery store over there even has one."

"Would this friend of yours be that blind chick that wanted a little girl to come over and read to her and hold her hand?"

"Well, forget it if you don't want to help me." Jeff found himself becoming very angry on account of Willie's denigrating comments.

"I didn't say that…" Willie screwed up his face. "Sure I'll help you, Jeffie! Let's see, what could you do for me?" He considered a moment, as if struggling to think of anything at all, then as if an entirely new idea had struck, "so, the grocery store doesn't have a Mad. Hmm. I betcha it'd have beer though. A six-pack of Coor's, maybe? Now **there's** something you can do for me! Tell you what. You get your blind girlfriend to find her way over to the store and get your pall Willie some beer, n'I'll see what I can do about finding her a Mad." He stuck out a sweaty hand.

Jeff shook, but had the sinking feeling that he somehow was coming out on the short end of the deal.

But, soon enough, the matter of a six-pack of Coor's was no longer the most troubling news he must bring Irene. After announcements, when the others were filing out variously to their classes, Ms. Larson gestured for him to remain.

"A word, Mr. McGowan?"

Jeff waited until the room had emptied, then, feeling as if things had gone far too well to be safe, stepped to the side of her desk.

"How goes it with our project?" his teacher asked.

"Fine, I guess."

"You guess?" She raised her eyebrows in mock alarm. "Did you tell her that you are a young man?"

Jeff felt his face burning with a sudden intensity, then realized, almost too late, that Ms. Larson must be joking. "She never found out," he answered solemnly.

Laugh-wrinkles deepened all over Ms. Larson's face. "I love it," she said. Seriously though, are things going alright?"

"Yeah, I think so. I've been helping her with her algebra," Jeff concluded helpfully.

"Whew, that's pretty impressive for a seventh-grader. Blind people don't always get the opportunities they should in education. It's really good of you to help out, Jeff."

"Oh, she knows a lot of things though." Suddenly, Jeff had gotten a glimpse of Irene as somebody stuck forever in Second Grade, and he hurried to erase the impression from his teacher's mind. "She designs clothes and everything."

"Well, that is amazing." This time she really was impressed. "I'm glad you told me about this. You see, we're all going to make a presentation right before spring break to show the school, and the community, generally what we've accomplished during this experience we're having."

A feeling of panic took possession of Jeff for the second time. "You mean, like a written report?" he asked, hoping against any reason for having hope.

"Well, no, actually, we'd like to work up a demonstration or a tour or a slide-show, or whatever might seem appropriate for the project in question. In your case," she smiled warmly as if bestowing a favor, "I thought that your friend-Irene might be willing to participate in our event with us. Now you've told me about her sewing work, which is really impressive. Maybe she'd consent to showing her creations."

"She doesn't get out much," said Jeff, feeling as if the battle were already lost.

"All the more reason to invite her, don't you think?"

"I don't know."

"But you'll look into it?" Ms. Larson was already picking up her attendance list for the next class. "If you can get around the handicap of not being a girl, I'm certain you can coax a lonely blind lady out into the social scene. Besides" -she leaned nearer, confidingly-"women love to be complimented on their cooking and their needlework. That, and babies. That's why I'm a teacher. I can't cook, I can't sew. And, I've got all you brats!" She opened a textbook and the interview was completed.

In the days that followed, Jennifer visited her Special Friend nearly every afternoon and she became both more used to, and more adept at, dressing the part. Jeff had observed that many girls wore their brother's white shirts to school, and this simplified changing somewhat. On days when he had gym, he brought a skirt, underwear, socks and sandals in the same bag with his P. E. outfit, changing when She reached Irene's. Jeff/Jennifer wondered sometimes whether there was any real point in changing at all, but the process seemed to make it easier to believe in Jennifer.

When they'd known each other about a week and a half, Jeff brought, along with his clothes, a piece of wire screen cut with his mother's pinking shears from an old roll he'd located in the garage. He also brought some nylon fishing line from one of Lorna's projects, and a large, heavy needle which their grandmother, he'd been told, had used for sewing feed sacks.

"Can I use your bathroom?"

Irene laughed. "Depending on what you want to use it for. My laundry's hanging all over, but I think that the crucial place is uncovered."

It took a few moments to change this time. Realizing that most people gave some evidence of having used the facilities when in there, Jennifer finally flushed the toilet, then, with the sink running, found the items for screen door repair.

"I wondered how I'd go about mending that hole." Irene had been delighted by the big needle it's very threadable eye. "This used to be my Aunt's house, so I don't even have a landlord to bitch at. At which to bitch!" She corrected herself with exaggerated care. "My Language teacher would have a holy fit. I came here so I could be near the technical college. My folks weren't all that happy about me leaving at home at all, and I sure didn't want to give them any more reasons to make the drive over than I had to."

They began, with Jennifer keeping a sharp eye toward the street, passing the needle back and forth. Irene was on the living room side of the screen door, sewing the little cut square of patch over the ragged hole.

"Speaking of things we aren't supposed to do and all that," Irene gave the needle a vigorous poke through a difficult place in the weathered mesh, "did you ask your friend about the Mad magazine?"

"Well, I did," Jennifer said uncertainly, "I have to do something for him before I can get the magazine."

"Oh, dear!" Irene was fully cracking up now. "Don't ever let yourself get put in that kind of position, girl, unless it's your idea in the first place."

Realizing what it must have sounded as if she was saying, Jennifer blushed deep red. "I didn't mean that!"

"I know. What is it the little pervert wants?"

"A six-pack of Coor's beer." Jennifer said it without thinking, then in spite of the impending refusal which was sure to come, felt relieved that at least it was out.

"Mmm." Irene wrinkled her forehead seriously. "That's a pretty sticky wicket. Contributing to the delinquency of a minor, possibly several, doing it in exchange for questionable reading material, not authorized by the National Library Services for the Blind. Setting a bad example for the young, for the community in general. It's a deal!"

"Really?"

"Sure." Irene stretched, before turning a corner and continuing up a vertical seam. "What are you? Twelve? Thirteen? About one can apiece is about average for that age. They'll either barf it up somewhere or make asses of themselves and fall asleep. Not that," she said confidingly, "it's any problem for boys to make asses of themselves anyway."

A movement in the corner of her eye made Jennifer fix attention again on the roadway, having allowed her vigil to lapse during their conversation. Somebody was walking there, turned so as to be staring pretty directly at the house. "Just a minute, Irene." Jennifer hurried past her into the safety of the living room. "I just want to see if all the stitches are going to hold."

"Oh, gee," Irene said scoldingly, "I'm a professional seamstress, or something, and you, a mere novice of at womanly arts, are going to critique my skilled craftsmanship. I'm quitting! No, wait a minute, I'm putting in for a raise!"

It was Willie. Forgetting about the screen entirely, Jennifer backed further into the concealing recesses of the living room.

"What's wrong?" Irene demanded. "Did you make a mistake? I know I couldn't have."

Irene's jocularity served to snap her back to the job at hand. "No," she said, "I thought there might be something. There isn't, though."

The screen door being an accomplishment now, Jen asked "Everybody seems to be so flabbergasted that you can use a sewing machine. Do most-well, blind women know how to do that?" (She still had trouble saying that word to Irene, though Irene had said on their second meeting "That's me. Blind as a bat. Calling it something else won't make the lights come on.")

"It's hard to say, really," Irene answered. "I went to the State School. Down there, they pushed gym, they pushed music, they made everybody take shop, and home-EC, no matter whether you were a boy or a girl. I showed some promise with an old Singer they had (the machine, not the choir director)." She guffawed, "And the teacher spent some extra time with me. I don't know what kids in regular public school get. As it was, a previous school I'd gone to, left me so far back in Math that I ended up in the Dumb Class and I wasn't setting the woods on fire in most of my other classes either. I didn't graduate until I was twenty, and my folks bought my sewing machine for me since it was about all I was any good at, I suppose, and to keep me out of their hair…"

"You didn't graduate until you were **twenty**--?" Jennifer tried not to let the horror she felt show in her voice. *Five years till I graduate, and that already seems like an eternity!* "How can that be?"

"You tell me, kid, and we'll both know," Irene said. "I recall though, that only a couple of the kids in my class were in the grade they were supposed to be."

Suddenly, Jennifer was rather sorry for bragging about helping Irene with their schoolwork. Imagine, having to get help with their assignments from-from a kid.

Now, Jennifer recalled guiltily that she still hadn't brought up the subject of Irene's possible participation in Community Services Month, rather than merely being a project herself, and Mrs. Larson would be expecting an answer sometime-- But, how to ask Irene?

"I don't suppose you'd like it much" she said, "if people wanted to come around, looking at your stuff and making a big deal about it?" Jennifer asked almost hopefully. "I mean, wouldn't that be like an insult?"

"If-" Irene answered slowly, "-I actually accomplish something-then I guess people can make as much as they want out of it, and with my sewing I accomplish something." Then, the solemn mood evaporated. "Fortunately, I'm a woman of varied talents. I can tie my shoes too!" She presented a somewhat disreputable sneaker, half-through at the toe.

This effectively changed the subject, leaving Jennifer feeling acutely chagrined, as her attempt to guard Irene's privacy seemed to have backfired. *(Maybe it would be good for Irene to come to school or some other place where people could look at her clothes designs and find out about the things she can do. Maybe Ms. Larson is right and that would be the best thing I could do for her. Only, how can I? How could I take her anyplace? She's the only one who knows-I'm 'me.')*

"Come meet Gussie," Irene had invited, when they were both thoroughly sick of nickel and dime algebra, on that first tense but fascinating afternoon. She'd led the way to the musty, bare-studded work area in the rear of the house. "A Sears industrial model," she said. "I could sew a pup-tent if I wanted."

Jennifer stepped forward, eyeing the formidable-looking black contraption with mingled awe and something like fear. "Neither Mom nor Lorna were ever much on sewing. I've tried, but just with a needle and thread. How does the needle go all the way through then come back?" She bent to examine the needle housing.

"It doesn't," Irene said. "Interesting thing, that. The needle just sort of pokes loops of thread through the cloth, then this part down here," she put her finger on the bobbin, "pokes loops through the loops on the other side of the material. Here, do you want to try?" She picked up a piece of blue denim from a pile of remnants lying on the old board and wrought iron work table, folded it. The sewing machine hummed and chattered, tingeing the air with the whiff of ozone. The scrap was now transformed into a tube, or sleeve. "Now you try."

"Do they make patterns that you can feel?" Jennifer asked.

"Sure." Irene went to a drawer, taking out a folded dress pattern embossed on heavy paper. "You can probably see the Braille markings." She indicated with her finger. "Like most anything else in Braille though, these cost a bunch, so I often take things apart and use them to make my own patterns for either part or all of a new thing I'm making." She returned to the sewing table to find a small pile of what looked at first like straps, but was actually a pair of pants disassembled into four parts.

Jennifer's own sewing lessons had begun thus, almost timidly, but had progressed in the intervening days, along with Irene's math and their mutual regard.

Jennifer gathered up the leftover fishline, dropped Grandma's needle back into the bag with the street clothes. "Looking good," she said to Irene.

"Who, me?"

Later, while the two of them sat over potato chips and chocolate milk. Still warmed by their success, Irene said "there's a real neat movie on this Friday. Have you heard of 'Wait Until Dark?'"

"No. What's it about?"

"Well, you see, it's about this blind woman who's got this murderer after her, and how she fights against him," Irene summarized. "The problem is, there are lots of places where all you've got is just that creepy mood music, and if you can't see, you don't know what in hell's happening. You see..." -she paused for dramatic effect- "...it's about a blind woman, but if you're blind you can't follow the story!"

"Oh really?" Jennifer answered, attempting to convey interest.

"'Oh really?'" Irene parroted. "Not even a 'that's too bad,' or 'something should be done about that?!' What I had in mind is, why can't you come spend the night Friday. It's not a school night, and we can watch it together and talk about girl stuff and just make a night of it?"

Jeff's steps were slow on their way home that evening. Seldom had he been in so many different sorts of trouble at the same time. It was particularly disconcerting therefore when he saw that his mother was waiting for him when he reached his destination. She was standing in the living room picture window, catching his glance almost as soon as he turned into their street.

"I'm glad you're home, Jeff," Mrs. McGowan said without preamble.

A chill ran through Jeff from his ankletted feet to his recently scarved topknot.

"There's a mother-daughter function at school this Friday."

And she's talking to **me** *about it?* Jeff knew he must be beet red and nearly laughed out loud with the irony of the situation, and the relief of finding out that he wasn't being cross-examined, yet. "So you and Lorna are going to go?" Jeff asked, not knowing what else to say.

"Well, yes." His mother answered. "I don't know the time to be nearly as involved with you kids and your schooling as I should, and Lorna is so, oh-- different and kind of standoffish. I thought we'd go to the doings, after an intimate little supper for two. That is, if-"

"If?" Jeff asked.

"I was just wondering if you could find a friend to stay overnight with, or maybe I should get a sitter for you?"

"Oh Mom, I don't need a sitter!" he protested.

"Now Jeffrey," Mrs. McGowan crooked an admonishing forefinger. "You know very well I don't approve of you being alone at night."

Suddenly, Jeff saw a solution, in part at least, to two or three of his current dilemmas in his mother's suggestion that he sleep over with a friend. "Let me work on it, Mom," he said. "Probably, I can stay at Willie's.

"That would be just fine, dear," said his mother. You're a big help." Then, when he thought the conversation had ended-- "May I ask, Jeff, what your sister's blue school dress was doing bunched up in your closet?"

Chapter 4.

Sleepover? Perhaps to dream.

This was one of those times it seemed to Jeff that someone besides himself was speaking. His lips, his tongue, his entire mouth felt perched to immobility and there was that coldness that near panic bestows. His voice sounded in his own ears very high in pitch and unfamiliar. The wonder was that Jeff, or whoever that was who was now speaking, could force out the words at all.

"I'm sewing Lorna a dress for her birthday," he heard himself saying. "I needed it for-for a pattern?" *No. She'll never buy that, but…*

"What a sweet idea, Jeff." His mother was laughing. "Didn't you know though that you had one of last year's dresses? She's grown since." Mrs. McGowan beckoned. "Come upstairs," she said. "I'll give you something that's the right size." She led the way up to Lorna's room.

"Here." Jeff's mother handed him a spring, floral cotton print on it's hanger. "Keep it hanging up," she ordered. "I don't suppose it'll be missed." She sighed. "I do wish your sister would take more of an interest in her appearance. Maybe your gift will be an inspiration for her." Mrs. McGowan didn't sound very hopeful, though.

Jeff's fingers nervously clutched the hanger hook as he brought it to his room, grateful his Mom had gone downstairs and was no longer watching him. *Imagine, having permission to keep a dress in your closet! Now, what the hell am I going to do about that birthday present?*

Jeff closed his closet, then his bedroom door, flopped on his bed, reached down a library book from his desk. He'd been keeping up with homework pretty well during the Study Hall and just now, he needed something other than more hassles.

Jeff's reading tastes usually ran to historical novels and sometimes a good science fiction book or collection of short stories. As Jennifer though, it was becoming clear that girls did more than dress. What did girls read, for instance? History, sure, and possibly the odd science fiction book, though SF seemed often to be in the boy's section of the school library. What else did they read though? He'd diffidently brought up the subject with Jennifer Wright at school one day, pleading a need to find some good books to read with Irene. "What kind of books would a woman want read to her do you suppose--?"

"What kind?" she had repeated, to see if she'd heard right. "I don't know, just books I suppose. Well, maybe books about romance, you know, boyfriends and stuff. Why don't you ask her?"

Feeling somewhat boxed in, Jeff had said "she just told me to pick out something good." Come to think of it, Irene had plenty of books, both in Braille and on Talking Book, which were boxes of records. But, the books weren't for Irene.

"Well, have you ever heard her talk about any book she has read?" Jennifer Wright inquired, in an effort to achieve some resolution to the difficulty. Susan was coming up, and Jeff was wishing that he hadn't engaged in the discussion at all. Still, Jennifer was looking at him in that way that suggested that the conversation wouldn't stop until she got some sort of answer.

"She told me once that she likes to read Mad magazines." That sounded a bit goofy, Jeff thought, so he asked "what kinds of things do you like to read?"

"Well-," Jennifer said again, "I like some of the classics, like Jane Eyre and Wuthering Heights-that kind of stuff. Right now, I'm reading True Grit. It's a story about a girl whose father is killed and she wants to get revenge against the killers. I think it's a movie too. You've heard the song on the radio, you know, Glen Campbell?" Suddenly, she stopped. "Oh, I'm sorry Jeff." At first it wasn't clear what was wrong, but Jennifer added "I forgot that your dad had died." She looked as if she'd committed something unpardonable.

"Aw, that's okay," Jeff said. People did that sometimes, acting like it'd happened just the other day, instead of way back when Jeff was still just a little kid.

Susan Manchester rushed in to fill the uncomfortable vacuum. "If she likes stuff like Mad Magazine," she told Jeff, obviously having picked up the gist of what was being discussed, "you should get this book called Ask Alice. I doubt they'd even let it in the library, but I'll lend it to you, if you want."

"Drop on by the library some afternoon, Jeff," Jennifer Wright said then, not to be outdone, and sounding Very Official. "We'll pick out some nice titles for your friend."

So, Jeff/Jennifer had ended up with Ask Alice, a book about a girl who had the same first name as Mom, but did things Mom would never even contemplate-as well as True Grit which turned out to be a kind of Western, and three other books which were judged adequate and interesting. *I should've asked Lorna. She'd have just chucked a Physics book at me and told me that's what girls read!* But, it was interesting, if sometimes a little troubling to read a novel through Jennifer's eyes.

That evening, Alice McGowan delayed her bombshell about the Mother-Daughter Fashion Show since Lorna seemed to have news of her own, which might (just possibly) put her in a more receptive mood.

"You see, there isn't any way for someone in a wheelchair to get up the library stairs," Lorna was saying, as she dug into their mother's rather hastily thrown-together meal of ground beef burgers with chips and supermarket salad. "I couldn't bear the thought of inventory and I'm no good at reading to little kids," Lorna added, around a bite of sandwich. "I think I got permission to look into the problem with the steps, just to keep me out of the librarian's hair."

"Surely," her mother expostulated, "you don't intend pouring concrete or something like that?"

"Of course not," Lorna replied. "Though," she said primly, "I'm sure I could if need be. No, the idea is really very simple. You make a ramp that has cleats on the bottom so it can lay on the steps and lock into them. Then you use a pulley arrangement to drive the wheelchair up to the door."

"Sounds dangerous, dear. Do you think this is really such a good idea?"

"Isn't ignorance much more dangerous?" Lorna asked what sounded like a clinching question. "Such as..." -she chewed for emphasis- "...might occur if the occupant of the wheelchair was unable to reach the library stacks?"

Mrs. McGowan brightened. "I'm happy you're so altruistic, dear," she said. "You won't mind learning about the spring fashions with me at Mother-Daughter night this Friday."

Lorna looked horror-stricken. "Oh, no!" she groaned. I'd rather read about the three bears to kindergartners!"

"Someday perhaps," her mother philosophized, "if you're going to be a professional woman like your dear old gray-haired mother, you may as well learn early how to dress for success!" Mrs. McGowan smiled benignly through her daughter's protracted shriek of indignation.

"So, since when is this Willie such a great buddy of yours?" Lorna had wanted to know, when all of the other arguments against going to the

Mother/Daughter night had been exhausted.

"It's very kind of his parents to offer-" her mother reprimanded, forgetting happily that no-one had offered, or <u>asked</u> for that matter.

("And just why should I?" Willie said, when Jeff self-consciously put the proposal.

"Because of the beer," Jeff said again.

"Yeah?" Willie demanded suspiciously. "What about the beer?"

It was after school on a day not scheduled with Irene. Jeff had been making a show of hanging around the building, hoping to deflect attention thereby, from those other times when fleeing any companionship he had slipped stealthily away from the school grounds, clutching his paper sack.

"I've got to get it with my cousins, see?" Jeff improvised. "We'll get the beer, but Mom won't like it if she knows I'm with them. They're a wild bunch, she says. It'd just be easier if Mom thinks I'm spending the night with somebody from school."

"What about your blind friend?" Willie countered accusingly. "Why can't she just get it for us?"

"Oh, you know-" Jeff replied. "She's afraid someday might find out, then the school might make trouble for her."

"How's anybody going to find out unless you tell?"

"No way special," said Jeff, "in fact she's giving me the money to buy the beer as long as my cousins pick it up."

"So you still want the Mad?"

"Sure I do…"

"Okay," Willie said. "Monday. You bring the brew, I bring the magazine."

"What about Friday night?"

"What?" Willy asked. "Oh, yeah. Anybody calls I'll say you're sleepin' over."

"How about your folks, though?" Jeff asked apprehensively.

"Ah hell," Willy guffawed. "They'll be passed out by ten. I'll tell 'em you're sleepin' over and they'll never know the difference."

Jeff didn't find Willie's assurance very reassuring, but it was probably as good as could be expected. His own mother wasn't exactly a detail person around home.

Suddenly Willie asked "Are you gettin' in her pants?"

"What!?"

"The blind lady. She can't get out much, even a fairy like you'd look okay to a blind chick!" Willy dug Jeff in the ribs and ran off.)

All had looked simple enough at the dinner table, with the argument between his mother and sister to shield Jeff from his own controversy and now, with Willie as an ally in deception, everything seemed to fit. Jeff had a place to go, Irene had somebody to watch the movie with, Willie his beer, Mom and Lorna their evening out. *What else can I do?* Jeff thought. *If I don't go to Irene's, I'll mess up things for everybody!* Then had come The Dream, and following The Dream, the cold morning light shed another complexion upon what he intended to do.

The dream had started like many before. Jeff was a girl. Everybody else knew it, and to start out, it was okay. He/she was wearing a dress that wasn't a hand-me-down from Lorna. It was a birthday present and the three of them, Jeff with Mom and Lorna were going downtown for something very special (though Jeff never found out what). They were in a department store when Jeff realized suddenly that (she) had to go to the bathroom.

At first there was no problem. The restrooms in the store were easy to locate. When Jeff was about to push the door open however, a sales-woman took ahold of Jeff's sleeve.

"Little girl," she said, "that's the wrong one."

Jeff looked up at the engraved door-plate and read "Men." Flushing with embarrassment, Jeff stepped leftward to the door marked "Ladies" which swung open suddenly and he was confronted again, this time by Ms. Larson, saying "Jeff, your project is way overdue and you've left your blind friend looking for the soap…"

Then, Irene, wearing a pair of granny-glasses and pushing a shopping cart, was anxiously crossing and recrossing the tiled floor, tapping with her cane as she searched for a wrapped bar of Dial, which each time, she managed to just miss.

Now, just as he was bending down to get the soap for Irene, Jeff noticed his dress was gone and he was in his school clothes, except the end of the nightgown was hanging out the back of his pants like a too-long shirt tail. The place was filling up now with women and girls, all talking loudly and wondering what a boy was doing in the ladies' washroom!?

Jeff had continued borrowing Lorna's nightgowns and this time it had hiked up above his waist, and he really did have to go! Jeff crept out of bed and was about to open his door and step out into the hall. Though he heard nothing, he hesitated. The dream was still on him, the feeling of discovery was strong. He slipped the nightgown off and got clean shorts and undershirt out of his drawer, pulling the shorts over the frayed bikinis he had worn under the gown. Suitably camouflaged, he crossed into the bathroom and locked the door.

Returning to his room, Jeff sat on the edge of his bed thinking about the dream and-everything. As long as he found a way to get the dress for Lorna, he didn't feel too badly about using her clothes. After all, if things were reversed, if Lorna was the little sister and Jeff the big brother, nobody'd think twice if Lorna wore her brother's jeans or something. And of course there was no reason to lie to Willie. Willie was a pig. Besides, Willie'd be getting what he wanted. Mom might not approve of his spending the night with Irene, especially without permission. But it was Irene herself who worried Jeff the most. Wasn't the lie he was telling her the worst of all? Wasn't Jeff somehow cheating her out of having a real girl to do stuff with?

Not really, argued the same voice who'd told him in the first place that it was okay to be Jennifer. *Nobody else was bothering with Irene, and if she knew you were a boy maybe she'd have refused you as a friend/helper. Don't you have fun together, and doesn't she enjoy having you visit at least as much as you like visiting her?* Well, yes, Jeff had to admit. So far, Irene had gotten what she'd asked for, and Jeff had gotten the chance to play at being a girl, something that had been fun and strangely exciting. But now things were different, weren't they?

Of course there had to be something pretty wrong at the base of what Jeff/Jennifer was/were doing because otherwise why would it be necessary to use such deception? *Secret agent*, thought Jeff, though this, he knew would sound just plain stupid to Mom. So he sat for he knew not how long, there on the edge of his bed, wrestling with it all. Yes, Irene was the one most affected by all of this. Somehow, she would have to be told. After that, other things would have to be done, but first Irene.

The interval of time separating this resolve with the actuality of doing it kept the idea from being too disturbing- lending, rather, a certain comforting sense that he was doing the Right Thing. Maybe now, he could sleep.

For a moment, Jeff eyed the gown which still lay on the bedside rug in an untidy heap of pastel pink, barely visible in the near darkness. At first he considered putting it back on, but decided against it, not entirely certain why. He did pick up the nightgown and fold it though, tucking it under his cold weather things in his bottom drawer. Sometime he'd probably want to again, he supposed, but that was okay. Sometime could take care of itself. Jeff slipped between the sheets.

Jeff's Midnight Interview with his conscience cost him his morning leisure. Sleeping through the alarm, he was startled awake by the arrival of the milk truck which usually passed him on the way to school. Jeff leapt from bed and practically vaulted into his clothes. He threw slices of cold cuts, bread, and an apple into a sack for lunch, disregarded breakfast, and with his change of clothes in the gym bag, ran from the house. (As it turned out, lunch was delayed as well.)

It was possible that left to himself, Jeff might have taken just as long to make the call, or might not have made it at all; but the need for haste he felt when at last his turn came to use the school's single pay phone nerved him to action.

Lunch period was nearly over when at last, the landing was cleared of loitering potential eavesdroppers. With a deep breath and a glance, first up then downstairs, Jeff sprinted for the booth.

"Hello?"

"Irene?" Jeff heard his voice again pitching toward shrillness.

"Jennifer!"

(This, with surprise. Good. She knew the voice and there was no need to further compound the lie.) "Yes. Hi Irene-sorry if this is a bad time to call."

"No, that's okay. Did you want to ask me something about tomorrow, or am I supposed to sign a pink slip for you?"

"It is about tomorrow-I didn't know for sure if I should come over or not."

"Oh, no!" Irene sounded genuinely disappointed. "Doesn't your Mom want you to come?"

"Well, not exactly." Jeff/Jennifer floundered for some way to lead into the heart of the matter. "I just thought that I should tell you about something."

"Oh really?" Irene chortled. "You haven't killed anybody?"

"No. You might be mad at me though." Jeff broke off. He wanted, both of them wanted, very much for Irene not to be mad.

"If you've robbed a bank" Irene was still laughing, "I'd only be mad if you didn't give me your cut for keeping quiet."

Jeff thought desperately about the impending end of lunch and the upcoming P. E. period. Still Irene was cracking jokes.

As if in response to the unvoiced panic Irene said "Listen honey. Can you come if you want to?"

"Yes."

"Do you want to, forgetting about your ugly secret I mean?"

"Well, yes."

"Alright then. At your age I baby-sat kids not nearly as much younger than me then, than you are younger than me now. Even if you are an escaped felon I can take care of myself. So come- if you want to."

Jeff was very much emptied now of anything to say and a silence ensued, emanating from both ends of the phone.

"Really," Irene said at last. "I'll be looking forward to it. We'll do our nails, and talk then." She chuckled, said good-bye.

She doesn't even wear nail polish, and she bites her nails! Jeff wondered just a moment why Irene had spoken just as she had, but only for a moment. *Oh no! It's time for gym and I've still got girl's underwear on!*

Dressing so hurriedly this morning, Jeff had pulled his pants on over both pairs of underwear, having left Lorna's bikinis on under his shorts. Not only had he missed breakfast and now lunch, he'd gone to the bathroom hurriedly at home and not since. When leaving the house his haste had been so great that he'd grabbed the bag of Visiting Clothes but had forgotten his Thursday Gym class. Jeff ran to the nearest boy's lavatory. Two guys were finishing up at the row of urinals. Jeff darted to one of the stalls (doorless like most boy's room facilities), dropped pants and underwear in a single movement and stayed seated until both urinals flush-hissed and the boys were gone.

He hastily removed his shoes, stepping out of his jeans, removed the shorts then the panties. At that moment, the restroom door *shooshed* again. Frantically, Jeff jammed both legs back into his pants, stuffing both pairs of underwear into the front pocket.

"Going barefoot, McGowan?" It was Willie.

Jeff nearly jumped out of his skin. What had he seen? "Had a rock in my shoe," Jeff said lazily, putting on the left shoe.

"In both of them?" Willie wanted to know.

"Yeah," Jeff said, putting on the right shoe.

"Better get your ass into gym," Willie warned. "You know how Mr.

Munger said he'd give you hacks if you were late again."

"Do you see a wallet over by the sinks, Willie?"

"No," Willie said, after a very cursory glance in the indicated direction.

Jeff used that opportunity to yank his pants up. "I think I dropped it someplace," Jeff told him, very conscious of the bulging pocket which stretched the left side of his jeans.

Willie tagged so closely that there was no time to make a ditch stop at his locker in the main hall. So reluctantly, though with haste, Jeff led off to Gym across the courtyard. He and Willie were the last two in the locker room.

As nonchalantly as he could, Jeff shucked out of his pants, getting quickly into his jock and gym-trunks.

Willie missed nothing. "Somebody steal your shorts, Sonny?" he asked.

"I got up late," Jeff told him, "and my Mom hadn't put the laundry away. I had trouble finding stuff."

"Dear, dear." Willie made sympathizing sounds with his tongue. "You are a mess."

After gym, Jeff finished up his penalty laps and returned now to a completely empty locker room. Emerging from the shower, he returned to his basket to find that his pants pockets had evidently emptied their contents in the metal drawer. Here was his change, his wallet, his comb and key chain-his shorts. He checked the left pants pocket. **Where were they?** His combination lock was lying inside the basket along with the other things, because he'd been intent on getting suited up and into gym.

He'd hoped to scarf some lunch on the way to Study Hall. His stomach ached with the extra exertion on top of the involuntary fast, but he'd better check around first. So Jeff spent a couple of minutes going around the rows of lockers and stacks of suit-basket drawers, giving the quick once-over to the clammy floor. Nothing. Finally satisfied for the moment at least, he grabbed his coat and headed out. If somebody found them in the hall or the courtyard or somewhere, the rumors would doubtless fly. But it wasn't as if anyone's name were in them....

At home that afternoon, Jeff continued to wonder whether he had let himself off a bit too easy where his sister was concerned. (Lorna did sound like Mom was dragging her off to the dentist with nothing to kill the pain!) Feeling a little guilty on her account therefore, and having nothing on of an incriminating nature (since before gym), Jeff invited himself to Lorna's room after dinner.

He sat on the bed and watched her glue another piece to the curious-looking structure which had nearly assumed it's final shape on her desk. Leaning forward to peer closer, he saw that it was a flight of stairs and some mechanical gadgets, possibly pulleys, suspended overhead from a dowel frame.

"You really mind going to that thing with Mom tomorrow?" he asked, after some moments of inner struggling.

Lorna sighed and laid down her glue-brush. "Oh- not really," she said. "I guess I don't do enough stuff with Mom. I just wish she wouldn't keep trying to push me into places I just don't-well, fit," she finished, trimming a bit of excess balsa with a hooked blade. "It's awfully convenient though," she added meditatively, "that you had to make up with that Willie Jackson brat just in time to have a fun place to go on a Friday night." She made 'fun' sound highly dubious.

Jeff held back an impulse to defend himself, finding the fact that Lorna was essentially *right* a matter of considerable irritation.

"Well," he temporized. "What's *wrong* with it, anyway?"

"Wrong with what? You having fun on Friday, or Willie himself?"

"No. I mean the fashion show thing Mom's all head up about."

"Oh--," Lorna twisted around in her chair to stare at her little brother. "Sometimes you are pee-culiar."

"What?" Jeff persisted.

"What what?" Lorna returned, showing her own defensiveness. "Ohhh," she shrugged, "I guess it's just that I'm afraid if I show the slightest bit of interest in anything, I'll wind up with it hanging on my closet rack next morning and then Mom will start trying to make a fashion plate out of me again. It's like she thinks she has to *civilize* me or something!"

"Don't worry," Jeff soothed. "We couldn't afford anything Mom would notice anyway, besides-you just have to look. I've gotta stay with Willie."

"And just why, exactly are you doing that--?" Lorna fixed her best accusing glare on Jeff.

"Why, just so you can be bee-utiful, Sis."

Jeff dodged the geometry book Lorna held poised for throwing. Now, it seemed, there really was nobody else to worry about except for Irene.

Chapter 5.

Wait Until: Wait Until Dark-Jen.

The day of the sleep-over was happily humdrum. There wasn't any need to pack stuff for school, since this was an Odd Day, no P. E. and he figured he'd better show up at home this afternoon in case something last-minute might come up. He ate his breakfast, packed an adequate lunch, and strangely unencumbered, walked to school swinging his lunch bag.

Excitement and anxiety still fought it out within him for first place in the emotional arena, but Jeff told himself that they had only till this evening (five, say, or five thirty), and everything would be settled one way or the other. He'd used a similar approach on tests before, and hadn't Jeff done his homework? At least he'd laid careful plans, hadn't he?

Thus bolstered, Jeff made it thought the day, even managing to successfully diagram a complex sentence that was tying his classmates in more knots than it had; earning him Miss Bulletin's tacit approbation. At the end of the day, when he peered into his reflection in the metal of his hall-locker, to see Jennifer peering anxiously back at him, "don't worry," he told her, "things'll work out okay."

But Things started to get a bit sticky that evening when his Mom declared that it would be the easiest thing in the world for her to drop Jeff at Willie's house on her way to dinner with Lorna. Fortunately, the matter came up early enough for Jeff to invent an (almost forgotten) late afternoon reading session with Irene. Fortunately as well, Irene's house was distinctly not on his mother's way to the restaurant.

Jeff escaped up to his room with his sleeping bag, where he considered the matter of attire. The upcoming conversation and the eventual possible outcome of the evening. He compromised on girl's underwear, his own school jeans and a T-shirt which could be worn by either boy or girl. He pushed a scarf, toothbrush, and a tube of toothpaste into his rolled sleeping bag along with his pillow. Then Jeff changed into neutral blue sneakers. After a sandwich and a bowl of chicken-noodle soup, he set out on foot for the meeting he both anticipated and dreaded.

"You've decided to stick it out with boring old Irene," Irene more said than asked.

"Mmm, well, I wanted to come," Jeff told her, feeling unfamiliar in his ambiguous status.

"Have we still got a problem then?"

Jeff's silence was betrayal enough.

Irene said quietly "Could it have anything to do with a curious little nickname some people call you?"

"What do you mean?"

"Jeff," Irene said.

"What did you say? How did you know?"

"All in good time." Irene wriggled a finger. "Don't spoil the narrative, girlie!" Unaccountably, Irene was laughing again. But after a while, so was Jennifer.

"Oh, I'm sorry," Irene said between chortles. "I noticed right away that you held a needle up and poked the thread at it. (Of course, everybody knows that a woman fetches the needle down to the thread.) I'd have given you something to throw, but I don't have any rats!"

"I throw like a girl anyhow." Jeff laughed with her, feeling unexpectedly wonderful with the secret finally revealed between them. "Come on, Irene, how did you know really?"

"Oh, at first I didn't," Irene said. "After a while, it just didn't matter. But, there were a few little things, I guess. Sweetie, in my day, a girl might bring pants to school and change out of a skirt afterward when she was going somewhere, but not the other way around. Somebody comes into your house in a pair of pants, heads for the bathroom, and comes out like little miss Muffet, you've got to be a little suspicious."

"But I thought you were blind!" It slipped out quite unbidden and Jeff felt his face getting hot.

"Oh, I am." Irene waved reassuringly. "But I can get little glimpses, sometimes when the light is just right, and these crazy eyes of mine are just right, or as right as they're ever going to get. About all I see is a bright color, say, or sometimes maybe a little bit of an outline. So, I noticed once or twice you had on different colors then when you came in, or I'd brush past and notice that instead of jeans, you had a skirt on. Stuff like that. Things didn't quite add up entirely, --and at this point I have a confession of my own, --I guess I peeked."

"What do you mean, you **peeked**?"

"It was really sort of an accident," Irene confided. "I was in the Little Girl's room when you were over once, and I happened upon a sack. It didn't take much to suggest to me that it was probably something of yours, because I was pretty sure I hadn't put it there, but curious me, I snooped. I've done laundry a time or two when I was growing up, and I'm afraid I know what jockey shorts look like. With the rolled-up jeans in the sack too, well it made a person think that was what you were wearing when you walked over here. I felt a little guilty about looking at your stuff, and I knew that you'd be embarrassed if I said anything, so I didn't."

"So I didn't do so well as a girl?" The disappointment felt like it would surely be showing up in Jeff's voice.

"Not that at all! I maybe shouldn't have asked for a girl in particular, but Junior High boys usually don't strike you as the sorts of people who will help a dumb old blind lady around the house. The real reason I didn't mention it was that by the time I suspected anything, I just didn't care--! As far as I'm concerned you're my old pal Jen and what you need to know is whether or not you want to show up in grubby dungarees, or a lace ball gown-- It's no skin off mine since I like you just because you're you. I suppose that sounds corny, but it's so, so there!"

Jeff/Jennifer felt tears in his/her eyes. Stumbling across the room, throwing arms around her friend. "Oh, I love you, Irene!"

Irene hugged back. "Me too, honey. Gosh, I'm going to have trouble remembering a new name to call you."

"Can you call me Jen….still….?"

"Jen it is! Get your butt in the kitchen, girl. I done went grocery shopping. I got graham crackers and marshmallows and Hershey bars and chocolate milk mix and cocoa puffs, oh yes, and your boyfriend's beer."

"Willie! He's not my boyfriend!" Jennifer asserted with indignation.

"Sure, sure." Irene brushed off the objection with mock disbelief. "That's what they all say. We're going to eat like pigs and hate ourselves in the morning!"

A sack of groceries sat on the counter by the sink. "First though," Irene said, pulling the flat, waxy carton from the sack, "how 'bout some pizza- just to keep us nutritionally balanced-" She went over to the stove, twisted the oven knob to the appropriate setting.

("See?" she'd shown Jennifer where grains of rice were Elmer's-glued to various places on the oven dial. "One setting for pizza, one for grilled cheese, one for brownies.")

They divided the pizza box to eat on, avoiding dishes to wash later, and dinner was served on Irene's tiny breakfast nook-table. Though Jennifer had eaten before, the sauce of worry relieved turned out to be relish indeed-or however that went--, and she munched contentedly, all questions laid to rest.

Then, suddenly, the most pressing question of them all, as it seemed just now, thrust itself forward in Jennifer's mind. "Irene, how did you know my name was Jeff?"

"Oh, that." Irene smiled. "Women's intuition. You'll have to get you some if you're going to keep on wearing skirts. No, really, it's just that I got a phone call from a very nice Teacher named...."

"Ms. Larson?!"

"Ms. Larson. Elizabeth, I believe."

"Oh, no!"

Irene held up both hands, palms forward, as if to stave off this fresh bout of hysterics. "Not as bad as it seems," she said. "You see, as I've said I'd had an inkling or two, and when she said 'our student who's been working with you,' well that narrowed things down pretty much. I avoided committing myself until she said 'Jeff' and 'he' and you seemed worried yesterday, so I put two and two together and got three X plus five Y or something, and your ugly secret is safe between us chickens."

"You're not old," declared Jennifer solemnly, "and you're a long way from dumb."

"Shut up and eat."

The telephone rang. "Hello?" Irene said into the handset, around a mouthful of pepperoni. "No, you must have the wrong number. She's not here." She listened for another moment, then, whispering in Jennifer's direction, "whoooops!" then to the phone, "hang on a minute, I'll go see. Who is this, by the way?" (To her companion, "Willie. That's the boy with the dirty magazines and the beer, isn't it?"

"Yes!" Jennifer gasped.

"He's asking for you."

"Asking for ME--? (Thinking a moment.) Better let me talk to him---"
Irene handed her the phone.

"McGowan, what are you doing there?"

Jeff answered automatically. "I had to do some reading for Irene."

Willie sounded suspicious. "When I asked If you were there, that blind
girl said that 'she' wasn't there. Why did she say that?"

"Must've been my sister she thought you meant," Jeff said weakly.

"So," Willie pushed on, "when're you going to get the beer?"

"It's all taken care of," Jeff told him, stalling.

"Alright then, when am I going to get it?"

"Monday, when I get the magazine." Jeff's more sensible nature took
over.

"Why not now?" Willie demanded. "Are you back from your cousin's?"

"I still have to do some reading for Irene," Jeff conciliated.

At Jeff's elbow "I **don't** want him over here!" Irene said.

"What?" Willie asked. "What did she say?"

"She says she doesn't want you over here," Jeff said, with only a twinge
of remorse.

"Only girls allowed, huh?" Willie retorted, and hung up.

"What in hell did he want?"

"Well," Jennifer said, with a long intake of breath. "Mom and Lorna
were going out, and I needed somebody to stay with. I knew I needed to talk to
you but I didn't know if you'd want me here after I had."

"I do see the problem," said Irene seriously. "I could be in a lot of
trouble though, because of this…"

"I could leave."

Irene thought for a minute. "Where does your Mom think you are, right
now?"

"Right now she thinks I'm here with you," Jennifer reassured her. "Later
on, I'm supposed to go over to Willie's."

"How did he get my phone number, I wonder?"

"I haven't got the foggiest idea," Jennifer said, a little indignantly. "No,
wait- your name and number were up on the board, I suppose it's been in my
notebook at school or maybe in my locker. I never thought Willie was smart
enough to think that up on his own. Or maybe he got your last name from the
teacher and looked you up in the phone book."

"Why would he call though? Did this Willie know that you were going to be here?"

"Not so far as I was aware," Jennifer answered. Then, very slowly, "come to think about it, he seems to follow me around a lot. Once I was over here and…"

"And what?" Irene prompted. "You saw this kid?"

"Uh-huh," Jen admitted. At the time, she hadn't been able to tell Irene about it, and Willie'd never said anything, so Jeff had decided that Willie hadn't recognized him that time when the two of them were working on the screen door. But now, she was just as sure that Willie had seen.

It was well after dark when the movie Wait Until Dark began. Armed with a pair of king-sized Pepsis and a foil-topped container of Jiffy Pop, the girls settled down to the TV and a quiet evening. The phone rang.

Irene reached for it. "Whoever it was, hung up," she said. "I sure hope **that** doesn't keep up all night long."

Phone calls and rowdy boys forgotten for a time, the movie broke in upon the nearly endless string of ads and public service announcements with the theme music of the Friday Show, and then it began inexorably to unfold.

"What's going on?"

"There's a lady with a doll. She's at an airport, but it doesn't look like she wants to take it through Customs or whatever, so she just gave it to that guy who she asked to hang onto it, so one of her kids wouldn't get jealous. So, now he's got it, and she took off…"

"Gosh, I'm glad you're over here," Irene said. "Tell you what, if any of this comes to light, so to speak, we'll just say that you heard there was going to be drinking at Willie's house, so I invited you to stay over here. I'd better meet your Mom sometime, too."

The phone rang. Irene reached for the receiver. After a second, "next crank call and I'll have a trace put on this line," she said.

"It's Willie," Jennifer observed, as if that were new knowledge. Jeff and Willie were not friendly enough to have memorized one another's phone numbers, but after locating Irene's directory during the commercial, Jennifer found the Jackson residence and dialed.

"Hello?"

"Hello, Mrs. Jackson, is Willie there?" He isn't? Sorry to bother you. Thanks." Jennifer hung up without identification. "He's not home," she announced with some surprise.

(Totally unaware of what he had, the man, a photographer, brought the doll home- leaving it with Susie, his blind wife in their apartment.)

"Oh-oh…" Irene said, enjoying herself immensely. "The plot is thickening. I can tell by the music. Is there anybody in the house yet?" And the plot is thick indeed--!

There's a doll full of drugs hidden in her house. They want it back and now, they've done murder too. Susie, the blind lady, isn't much like Irene, Jennifer decides. She's always apologizing about being blind, but she's pretty smart in a kind of haphazard way. With the help of a little girl (would I ever have that kind of guts?) *Susie has discovered that a string of phone calls (supposedly from the Police and somebody who claims to be her husband's friend)-are phony, coming from a booth across the street. And now they know that she knows!*

(In their own community, across another street-this one fronting the public library-another, less intentional but potentially catastrophic drama is, as Irene and Jennifer watch their movie, about to unfold.

In the park, near the center of town, with the hulking wood and concrete bleachers of the ball field as windbreak and shielded from casual view by a curbside screening of ornamental trees and shrubs, a small, variously burdened group of boys laid out a pattern in dried sticks and scavenged lumber yard remnants. Nothing about their effort is likely to be found in either Scout manual or fire marshal regulations, but they are enthusiastic. A match flares, then several more. So far, the boys have only a choking mess of acrid smoke.

"Hand me the can," the boy presently holding the matches demands.

A younger kid picks up the oblong can of lighter fluid and hands it over. The fire flares yellow as the aromatic liquid ploops onto the snapping, crackling sticks.

"Keep an eye out for fuzz," somebody says to no one in particular.

"Hell," said the eldest kid contemptuously. "They're all over at the station drinking coffee! Let's go find more stuff to burn."

Jeff could well appreciate Irene's point about the movie featuring a blind person being inaccessible to the blind. Large portions of it were entirely mood music, punctuated by crashes, footfalls, intakes of breath (gasp!), and the occasional shriek. (*A good thing I am here,* Jennifer decided, *the music alone would sure give* **me** *the creeps!*)

During the station break just before the climax, Jennifer hurried to the bathroom, switched on the light at a whole arm-length distance from the darkly-yawning aperture, finally managing to close the door behind her. Irene's smudged cabinet mirror with it's hairline fractures threw back eerie distortions of her own face and already-troubled expression. What would it really be like to be that blind woman in a pitch-dark apartment, with a murderer---? For a moment, Jennifer tried closing her eyes, but they popped open again in half an instant and she fled the rush of the suddenly flushing toilet for the welcome light of the front room. On one hand, she reflected, it was downright silly to scare yourself like that-but on the other, it was quite a bit of fun.

He was in her house---. She'd managed to smash out all the lights, but he'd chained the door shut and retaliated by spreading gasoline around, threatening to torch her apartment. She's spunky though, and armed with a kitchen knife, prepares to defend herself.

Though she would be on equal terms with this homicidal maniac with the sadistic sense of humor, he's opened the refrigerator, showing a light that most blind people would never think of--- and he seizes her! He drags her into the bedroom, and she plunges the kitchen knife into her assailant. (Only--- he refuses to die!)

It is now that Irene, and Jennifer too, hear stealthy and very real footsteps in the yard outside.

Chapter 6.

Watching You!

Over steaks and salad, attempting to capture the spirit of mother-daughter dialogue, "how's your project coming at school?" The question seemed merely one in a long chain of repetition. Lorna was focused too much upon mechanics as it was. *And here I am, feeding into that,* Alice reproached herself. To her surprise, though, Lorna didn't embark upon a set of statistics and design specs.

"I'm wondering about Jeff and **his** project," Lorna said, mopping a slice of egg-toast in the steak juice left on her plate. "Isn't he with her an awful lot, lately?"

"Do you think there's a problem with that?" Lorna's mother asked, betraying in spite of herself the extent of her own (till now) half formed concern on the subject.

"Oh, not a problem." (Alice winced as Lorna crammed in half a slice, continuing to talk around it.)
"Just that Jeff is usually by himself so much of the time, that it's really nice that now he's got a friend and something to do. That's all I meant."

"But isn't there something a bit strange about a boy, twelve years old, having so much to do with a woman who's in her- what- twenties? Thirties?"

Lorna considered that, slowly shaking her head. "Oh, I don't know, Mom…" She forked up a load of tossed salad, swimming in Roquefort. "Probably my best friend at school is the Physical Science teacher."

"But at least you don't spend all your time over at Mr. Deasner's house…!" She sipped at her de-caf and exhaled wearily. "I'm a failure as a mother," she declared.

"Not a bit," said Lorna indignantly. "You've got two socially aware children, neither of which has ever done drugs, blown up a train station or been indicted by a congressional sub-committee. You don't have anything to worry about."

Mrs. McGowan smiled a little sadly. "Here I went rushing off, allowing my son to arrange a night's accommodations without checking anything myself. What kind of a mother does that?"

"One who gives her kids credit for having some basic common sense," Lorna told her. Lorna was glad enough to have the conversation directed away from herself, but she felt a bit alarmed without knowing why, about the way the evening had started out where her brother was concerned. Wasn't Willie Jackson the kid at school who was always tormenting Jeff? Out loud she said "Well, if you're bothered, Mom, maybe I'd better call over there and find out how things are."

"That's a good idea. I'll go do that now, before we leave." Mrs. McGowan set down her coffee and half-rose.

Her daughter reached across the table to put a restraining hand on her shoulder. "I said I should, not you." *I had to open my big mouth,* thought Lorna. *Now let's see if I can get out of this.* "Seeing as Jeff's already there," she told her, "If you go checking up on Jeff, it's likely to ruin him socially. If I, as his sister, call though- that's another story. His friend may not even know I'm related to Jeff, and will assume that he has an extremely attractive girlfriend." (Lorna knew where her mother's buttons were, in spite of her general refusal to be conventionally girlish.) "You go pay the check," Lorna said, as the concern on her mother's face subsided somewhat. "I'll call."

Alice accepted a half-cup refill and lit a cigarette, (of which her children disapproved), taking guilty pleasure in the first deep lung-full. If some girls were flowers, she decided, Lorna was some kind of weed-wild and rangy, yet spicy, like prairie sage, and more impressive than beautiful. She patted at her lipstick with an apple-green tissue and examined her meticulous crimson nails. She puffed out the smoke, watching her daughters chestnut hair (lush, but unruly) cross the restaurant. *Probably a lot like me when I was that age*, Alice reflected. *Before... well, when I was still a girl.*

Jeff was another matter. Where Lorna was stubbornly persistent and always out-of-step with other people in that way that made **them** run to catch up, Jeff was-just out of step. Withdrawn, shy, yet self reliant, it was hard to figure out what made the boy tick. Not that his marks were anything to complain about, or that he'd ever been in any sort of trouble, like that Willie and his brothers-still, you could only wish that Jeff wasn't as much the recluse.

So, why do I have this feeling about this-blind woman? Alice wondered if the Strangeness really lay in the woman's age, or that Jeff, for a change, had something to do which wasn't up in his room or off in some solitary walk? *I've got to go make this Irene's acquaintance,* she decided. *First chance I get.*

Alice opened her compact to check her eye makeup and her orthodonture. Again, she exhaled tension and the general sense of not- inadequacy, to be precise, but embattlement? Was that a word? *Lots of things I should be doing with and for these kids- both of them, but where's the time? Where is the **time**!* She sprang (though with grace) to her feet. *We'll surely be late!* She waved for the check. *Good kids. Just not enough time for being just a mom since James passed away, leaving two children-three and five-and I had to go back to work.*

"Hello, Mrs. Jackson. Is Willie or Jeff there please?"

"Oh, is Willie playing with Jeff this evening?" The somewhat bleary voice on the other end of the phone inquired. "Another young girl- I think it was- called for Willie a little while ago, but he's out with his brothers."

"No problem," Lorna told her. "He must be at another friend's house. Thanks." *Damn the kid! What should I do now? Well, I bet I know where he is. He probably thought that Mom would have some kind of problem with his spending the night with his blind friend. With most kids that'd be a little weird, maybe, but Jeff isn't most kids. Better keep mum to Mom,* Lorna decided. *Don't want her going off again about forcing Jeff into the Boy Scouts or military school or whatever! Why can't Mom just quit worrying about us all the time?*

Lorna flipped down the phone book again, but knew it was futile. *Irene, she thought, Irene, Irene, what was her last name? Not under B for Blind or anything, that was sure.* If it wasn't Friday night, maybe Lorna could figure out some way to find the phone number. *Forget it for now, though.* "It's all because of this stupid fashion-dessert thing we have to go to," Lorna said aloud, slamming shut the phone book.

Rejoining her mother at the cash register counter, Lorna said, sincerely enough "Jeff's at his friend's house. He's doing fine."

(Once more, he'd come after her, a nightmare from out of the dark. But she manages, somehow, to reach the cord of the refrigerator and when the police arrive, along with her husband and Gloria-her
brave little friend who has gone for help-they find him dead and her squashed behind the refrigerator, crushed by fear, but victorious at last!) And....

The feet-scrunched in the weedy side yard, stepping on something that **cracked!** Like shattering glass and somebody cussed. Then the steps continued around the back of the house.

"Oh God!" Irene leapt from the couch. "I don't know if the back door's locked." She charged into the gloomy back recesses of the old house, and Jennifer heard the rattling of a latch and then a chain. "Our rear's secure," she announced, re-emerging into the front room. As if to validate her assertion, somebody rattled the back door (giggles), and the somebody dismounted the step.

At first, Jen had been terrified, partly under the influence of the TV. Then she recalled the various deeds committed by Willie, over the last couple of days, and now these sneaky footsteps--serious enough, but for the moment, push back to third place in the agenda of anxiety.

Jennifer stole from the couch and peeled back the drapes just enough to see out. "That's Willie and his stupid brothers," she muttered angrily, feeling herself largely at fault for the offending presence. "I'm going to go tell him off!"

"No," Irene said, "I think I've got a better idea."

From outside came "We want our beers!"

Irene rose.

Well tuned into the movie climax, she assured herself the other door was locked and chained. "Pardon me," she said, turning off both the light switch by the door, then signing for Jennifer to reach over and twist off the lamp. The living room was now lit only by the glow of the TV screen. "Blind people live in dark houses," she told Jennifer. "Or hadn't you heard. It seems to scare piss out of sighted people, anyhow."

"We want beers!" came, somewhat less stridently, from outside.

"The police please," Irene said, in voice calculated to carry, as she pantomimed a phone receiver. The commercial was on now, and the voices were receding.

"Got your dress on, McGowan?" a boy's voice jeered in retreat.

"Will they be back, do you think?"

"Couldn't say," said Jennifer quite frankly.

"What's his whole name?"

"Willie. Willie Jackson."

Irene flung open the window. "Your mother's looking for you, Willie Jackson!" she shouted. "Now," (to Jennifer) "Let's have some fun. I don't want to be made out a liar."

"What are you going to do?" The ending commercials were still on.

"Is there the name of a woman in school who works in the office, say, a secretary, or a counselor, even a custodian or something as long as it's a woman?"

Jennifer thought a moment. "There's Miss Lambee," she said. "She's the seventh-grade counselor."

"Perfect! Do you know her first name?"

"Diana."

"Great. Now what's the little pig's number?"

In no doubt as to which pig might be meant, yet alarmed all the same, "What are you going to do, Irene?!"

"Give, girlie. I'm hot now."

Apprehensively, Jennifer gave her the number.

(About this time, the bonfire has reached respectable size, taking most of it's exuberance out in poppings and crackings, but now again tossing large sparking embers up into the changeable night wind. One of the boys leans over to warm his hands over the fire, then, remembering the can of lighter fluid, squirts the oily substance (this time from respectful distance) into the flames which leap gratifyingly, now blue instead of yellow.

"Wait a minute," one of the other boys says, "I've got an idea."

The boy who's just spoken takes off at a sprint to rummage a nearby garbage can belonging to a residence whose people seem to be safely away, for all of the lights are out and no car is in the driveway. In a couple of minutes he is back with what he was looking for.

"Watch this," he says, pitching the empty spray can into the center of the fire. For a time nothing happens at all. "Get back," he cautions.

KABOOM! The can ruptures, residual antiperspirant belching a flare of purple, lacing the air with the acrid odor of combusting alcohol and perfume.

"That's **neat**!" This is the general consensus. Emboldened by so far not being disturbed or discovered at their incendiary play, the boys fan out to search other garbage cans, unattended garages, trash piles.)

"Good evening Mrs. Jackson? Yes, this is Diana Lambee from school. I'm sorry for calling so late, but I happened to be catching up in my office and I heard some children making a great deal of noise around the playground. I'm sorry to say, but they appeared to be drinking, and one of them was your Willie. Yes, I am terribly concerned and thought I would call you and let you know. Yes, I'm very sorry too." (Irene was restraining laughter, hopping from foot to foot in an effort to contain herself.) "Yes, I'm sure there's no need for you to come in on Monday. I'm working after hours, and there will be nothing on Willie's Formal Report. All right then. Good-bye."

They exploded into gales of giggles. "You haven't even seen the best part yet," Irene finally choked out. She went into the kitchen, removed the six-pack of beer from the refrigerator, crossed the living room to the door which she opened, and set the six-pack on the porch. "Self-administered punishment," she announced proudly. "They stay away and they can probably clear themselves. They come back, they'll take the beer and drink it, puke all over, and get their butts beat!"

"You're a genius, Irene!" Jennifer said, with a mixture of fear and awed admiration. In the back of her mind she knew that Willie would make her pay.

"Hey," said Irene, "I knew that!"

With the movie over, and excitement diminished for the moment "is that why that kid is giving you so much trouble, Jen?" Irene asked, "because he saw you wearing a dress?"

"He may have--." Jennifer told her then about the time she had seen Willie from the road out front, while the two of them were conducting screen-door repair.

"And he's evidently going through your things at school, if that's how he found my phone number."

"I'm really sorry, Irene…."

"Don't let it bother you, kid. I think you'll find that we weren't the ones who watched the scariest movie tonight."

The evening dessert and fashion-show drug on and on, and it was after eleven when Mom and Lorna finally got home. Paranoid that her mom was going to start in again with something silly like driving over to check on Jeff, Lorna hung around downstairs, her mouth still smarting from the aftermath of the lemon-meringue-and something called an Early California Strawberry Parfait-which, had seemed to Lorna like biting into a frothy, pink cloud.

Mom got into her robe and slippers though, settling down with the several newspapers she read, seemingly clear through, and Lorna could now go to her room to do her own worrying. She scooted her desk chair over to the window, though of course there wasn't anything to see this late and this season, but it was fun sometimes to just stare out into dark and imagine…

Except tonight, it was kind of hard to look out there and not be thinking about her daffy kid brother-out there, very definitely **not** spending the night with Willie Jackson. That story had more holes in it than a moth-eaten overcoat in a hail of bullets! *And it wouldn't have flown at all if it hadn't been for inconveniencing me!* Lorna decided, with justifiable pique. *Well-where else.*

Lorna switched on her bedroom light to inspect the model glued down on a scrap of plywood, ready to be transported first to Mr. Deasner, then to the Parks Department engineer who'd agreed to act as technical consultant on her Wheelchair Project. It seemed in good order. Even the little pulleys, made of brads and cardboard and slices of wine-bottle cork, turned-sort of, and the little balsa wheelchair actually moved. *I wonder if I should have made it to hold a Barbie, or maybe a G. I. Joe? Ah, to heck with it, it's done.* Lorna yawned, stretched. *I could go over and look for Irene's number in Jeff's school notebook.* For a moment she seriously considered doing that, but maybe it was best not to borrow trouble until you had to. She pulled out her pajama drawer, recalling that a lot of her stuff seemed to be getting lost lately. "What is it with the wash around here?" Lorna pulled on the oversized Huskies T-shirt and crawled into bed.

"Did you bring P. J. s?" Irene inquired, a while later.

Jennifer realized suddenly that even though providing herself with sleeping bag and the minimum needed to pass as a girl (at least in a blind person's house?), she'd forgotten about that! "I'm afraid I didn't, Irene."

"Now listen here," said Irene, adopting a scolding professorial tone, "you're going to have to get into the habit of lugging around a couple bagfuls of make-up and curlers and all sorts of improbable things that you might never use, but have to own anyway! For the present though, do you want to borrow a nightie?"

Jennifer found herself hesitating. It was one thing to plunder your sister's dresser, that being merely a borrowing of things from home. To put on things that belonged to somebody else, when she knew about it, wasn't that a different thing? "Gee, I don't know if I should…"

"I'm not going to argue about it," Irene said, yawning. She went into her bedroom, rummaged a while, and came back with a long, faded green flannel gown which she tossed on the couch. "There," she said. "You can use that or sleep in your BVDs. I'm throwing my sleeping bag over here by the kitchen-it's closer to the food."

Pretty sure now that the Willie problem was temporarily over, the two settled down in their bags. The soft flannel nightie smelled like Irene, sort of a mixture of books and plain soap and water and old furniture and leftover bakery goods.

"No fair going to sleep."

Jennifer wondered if sleep would even be possible this night. "Girl talk?" she asked, feeling just a little silly having said that.

"You've got it."

"Does your mom or sister have any idea at all about what's going on?" Irene asked at one point. "About the clothes and stuff, I mean."

"I-don't-know-"

"You use your sister's things?"

"Yeah, mostly."

"And she hasn't found things missing, or something?" Irene wondered.

In truth, Jeff had been finding it necessary to do the laundry most of the time lately, to guard against such an eventuality. Neither Mom nor Lorna had objected to having their stuff washed, dried, and neatly folded when they got home from work or classes. "I did almost get caught once," Jennifer confided.

"Oooo, that sounds good," Irene said. "Just a minute." She slid out of bed, slapping bare feet on the kitchen floor, helped them to two more cans of pop from the fridge. "Tell," she said, when tabs were pulled.

Jennifer recounted the incident of the blue dress and the birthday present which was now expected by Mother.

Irene guffawed. "Serves you right... Funny how things work out though. You see, to pursue my studies in clothing design, I get some money from the state for readers and helpers, and a bit for supplies. Since I need a project, your sister needs a dress and you're on the hook, you see how it all comes together. Is your sister about your size?"

"Well, close," Jennifer told her. "Taller, and she-she no longer wears under shirts."

"Aha! Well, what I've got in mind might serve a variety of purposes. You see, if anybody's going to take me seriously, I have to create something really original or something that people perceive I should know about.

"What people assume I know about," Irene went on, "Is 'handicapped people,' not just blind people, but anyone who has a handicap. There's not a whole lot of need for special clothes for blind people, maybe Braille day-of-the-week underwear or something, that's about it-- Take another group though, one with more physical problems, folks in wheelchairs, say. We might well be able to come up with a whole bunch of stuff to help **them**."

"My sister," said Jennifer, "is working on a project for people in wheelchairs too." She went on to explain Lorna's project.

"Really?" Irene was incredulous. "This is coming together in interesting ways. Would Lorna be open to a modeling show on innovative clothes for disabled people?"

"I don't know," Jennifer said doubtfully. "She's not really into clothes very much."

"What is she into then?" Irene asked.

"Solar energy."

"Solar energy?"

"Yes," Jennifer told her. "She wanted to build a solar pool heater for Community Service Month, and she's always trying to build methane digesters to take care of dog leavings, or build a neighborhood food dryer to dehydrate windfall apples. She's a solar energy nut, and if it doesn't look like a roll of aluminum foil or a black box with glass on it she's not interested."

"Hmmm," said Irene, a germ of an idea coming to her. "Would she work with us if we could give her a chance to get solar energy into the lime-light, so to speak?"

"I'd imagine…" Jennifer said.

"Okay, how about this?" Voicing the ideas as they came, Irene began sketching out a rough but plausible plan.

When, in an hour or so, sirens lanced their anguish through the still night, they paid no particular attention save to note-as people will-that somewhere, the peace is being shattered. Such things seemed far from where they were, remote indeed, while perhaps the strangest slumber party ever, continued as anticipated far into the blinking hours of dawn.

Chapter 7.

In the Sobering Light of Day

As it turned out, nobody got much sleep that night. When Jeff bid Irene a lukewarm good-bye, after a somewhat chilly breakfast, he'd trudged glumly home only to spy Lorna as he rounded the corner onto their block, waiting for him in the front yard. She was glaring up the street at him, nervously alternating from one foot to the other, occasionally throwing an anxious glance backward at the draped front room windows.

"Great!" Jeff muttered, shifting his bundled sleeping bag from his right shoulder to his left and going to meet her, showing entirely more bluster than he felt. "What are you looking at?"

"Never mind about that," Lorna retorted. "What's the idea of telling everybody you're in one place then sneaking off somewhere else?"

"How did you know?" Jeff flared, surprised into truthfulness.

"Partly," she said, with that supercilious big-sister tone Lorna used sometimes, "because nobody in their right mind could imagine you and Willie spending more than fifteen minutes together without you coming away with your feelings hurt. I didn't say anything, because I didn't want Mother getting all bent out of shape, but last evening she was getting all guilt ridden because she hadn't sent over a house-plant to say thank you to Mrs. Jackson, or personally packed your jammies, or checked whether you were safe. So I called Willie's, and-you weren't there."

"Okay, so what?"

"So what is that Mother is in there talking to your friend Irene on the phone. I'd hurry up and get in there if I were you."

It was as if a booted foot had suddenly landed in his stomach, so strong was Jeff's feeling of betrayal.

Even after her friend had at last drifted off to sleep around 5 o'clock, Irene had continued to toss and turn on her living-room rug. Things had just gotten too complicated, too fast, she decided, though that didn't really excuse anything. *I should have known, should have checked with Mrs. McGowan, but*

I didn't.

In actual point of fact, Irene had assumed, innocently enough that Jen/Jeff had squared things at home before calling her from school on Thursday. But, looking at things in the uncharitable light of your own conscience, it wasn't too hard to see how somebody could get the wrong idea about what was happening. Irene wearily shouldered her own proper share of the blame, but some of the responsibility must belong to Jennifer too, mustn't it? *You're the adult, aren't you.* Irene sighed. *Guilty as charged.* She tried every position she could to get comfortable, even lying finally on her stomach, but never did more than doze.

"I just don't know any way around it," Irene said, spooning up cornflakes and banana slices. "I've got to talk with your mom."

"How come?" Jennifer demanded, outraged. "Everything turned out okay. Nothing bad happened. And-I wouldn't want to worry Mom."

"Yes, I agree that nothing really <u>wrong</u> happened in the sense that we were here just watching a movie and having fun, but it wasn't fair for us to deceive your mother the way we did. I should have been more responsible. To tell you the truth, it was such a *riot* last night that I guess I forgot I'm a grown-up and I'm sorry about that, but we both have to try and be responsible."

I've never heard Irene talk that way before... The discordancy jangled within Jennifer. *Next thing you know, she'll be telling me to join Little League, or-read Boy's Books...* "Well, I didn't know what to do," Jennifer said, close to tears. "I thought that you thought I was a girl, and how was I s'pose to tell Mom that--? But you wanted me to come and I wanted to, and we HAD to talk about stuff and..." She broke off all of a sudden. "You aren't going to tell Mom about THAT!?"

"Oh God." Irene reached around the corner of the table, squeezing her friend's arm. "I'm not going to tell anybody <u>anything</u> except what I have to, meaning that you were over here last night. If your mother had known that Willie and the other boys were drinking, I'm sure she'd rather you were over here than with them."

"What she'd rather do," Jennifer said, getting up from the little table, "is to leave me with a babysitter!"

Sadly, Irene listened to her getting ready to go. It was probably just as well, Irene supposed, that she hadn't asked too pointedly about what Mrs. McGowan had or hadn't been told before. It was really too late to do anything other than what they had, and the kid must be feeling terribly alone right now.

She thought then, and not for the first time, about Boarding School and about Charlie. While Irene couldn't be certain exactly how closely Jennifer/Jeff's situation paralleled Charlie's, she suspected that she had some insight at least into what might lie in store for this very singular young person, trying so hard to cope in a world of unforgiving categories.

"Tell you what," Irene said, as Jennifer was rolling the sleeping bag. "You go home and talk to your mom, then call me. I won't do anything until I hear from you. Okay?" (Here I go again.) "So long as Willie keeps his big mouth shut, we could just say that you came to my house because you wanted to stay out of trouble, and weren't sure how to contact your mom or sister and didn't know what else to do.

Jennifer replied noncommittally, left for home.

"Well Stanley," Irene said aloud to the silent room, "it's a fine mess you've gotten us in <u>this</u> time."

By the time Lorna had confronted Jeff with his own waywardness, he'd already pretty much admitted that a plan of such complexity as he'd formulated over the past couple of days, was altogether too likely to fail in all sorts of ways. Maybe Irene was right when she said it was better to tell Mom at least part of what had happened. That made it hurt all the more to find out that Mom and Irene were already talking to one another, even as Jeff was making his gloomy trek from one to the other.

What Jeff couldn't possibly have known though, was that it was his mom who'd made the call. Alice McGowan, herself not enjoying the best of nights, had arisen early for a Saturday morning. Without Lorna's permission, she had gone through her son's school binder and the little address book, which he kept meticulously updated, in his pen and pencil case.

On the I-page she found Irene Carrol, with address and phone number, and a little notation that said 'Jennifer's best friend.' Alice wrinkled her forehead for a moment, puzzling about who this Jennifer might be, but not for too long. *I'll wait till ten,* she decided, *then I'll call.*

Irene stood, stretched, let her arms fall back to her sides, then smacking her fist into the other palm, emitted an "oof!" of frustration. *Am I really so lonely that I have to enable a twelve-year-old kid to do something just about anybody else in the whole wide world is going to call Perverted, just so I can have a friend?* Still, that was silly. Irene was selective in her choice of acquaintances, not lonely, as such. And she and Jen/Jeff? did have great times together.

As Charlie had found, the world can be such an <u>excluding</u> place. *Do I have to make Jeff/Jennifer's isolation complete? Isn't it okay for <u>her</u> to have a few hours a week to dress up and giggle and talk girl-talk? Who's really to say?* As she was formulating her own overture to Jeff's mother, whenever that should take place, she was jarred out of her brooding and nearly out of her shoes, by the querulous shrill of the phone, which-just then in her pacing-had drawn up about abreast of her.

"Hello?"

"Hello, Miss Carrol, Irene?"

"Yes."

"This is Alice McGowan. I believe that you and my son are-ah-acquainted?"

Well, speak of the devil! "Oh yes, Alice. How do you do? I was just about to call you. Jeff's just left." *Liar!*

"Oh? Well, great minds and all that-I should be expecting him home soon then?"

"Yes," Irene said, trying frantically to keep hold of what she was and was not supposed to say. "His friends seemed to be getting a little rowdy last night, so he called and asked if he could stay with me a while. We got watching a movie together, and I'm afraid we sort of passed out in front of the television." *There, that was all true-technically.*

"I hope my son wasn't pestering you or anything," Alice McGowan said, sounding not particularly discomfited by the news.

"Oh, of <u>course</u> not. He's welcome any time, night or day." Irene laughed.

"Here, I believe," Alice confided, "he comes now," as Jeff's announcement, followed by Jeff himself came sailing down the hall toward his mother's office.

(Though Jeff, walking home had nursed a grudging intention to inform his mother concerning the truth of his whereabouts, it was nevertheless just as well that Lorna had prompted him. For her warning fixed, if not the occurrence itself, at least the timing and somewhat, the structure of the admission.)

"Mom," Jeff called, jamming his sleeping bag into the hall closet and hurrying toward his mother's office, "Willie and the kids were drinking, so I went over to Irene's." The steady modulations of his mother's voice issuing through the half-open study door indicated that she was on the phone, and Jeff generally found that a confession blurted out when Mom was on the phone was likely to be a bit less damning than if delivered, so to speak, in Cold Blood. "I got back as quick as I could-" he added, in hopeful mitigation.

"So I've just been hearing," his mother called from within.

The women spoke perhaps twenty minutes longer, at the end of which it had been agreed that Irene would join the McGowans for dinner the evening of Wednesday next. *This Irene person seems normal though,* Alice reflected, during an interval when the other woman was talking. *Not like I expected-what did I expect?*

For nearly five minutes, Jeff stood as near as he dared to his mom's door, awaiting the clack of the receiver being put down and the eruption of displeasure that was sure to follow. As they talked, however (and talked!), Jeff, peeved at least enough for two, took himself upstairs.

"Hi," Lorna said, looking up from her book which she wasn't really reading, to see Jeff lingering in her doorway. "Come in."

Jeff half-sprawled on his sister's bed. Neither of them said anything for a minute.

Then, "I didn't squeal on you, you know," Lorna stated flatly.

"I know," Jeff said. "And Irene said she wouldn't-yet!"

Lorna pursed her lips. "I don't think she did either, Jeff."

"How do you know?"

"Mom called her," Lorna replied.

"Why?"

"I suppose Mom just thought it was time she got to know this gal her kid's been spending so much time with. That's all."

Another minute elapsed before Lorna, speaking slowly, reasonably, asked "what's all this about, Jeff?"

"What's what about?"

"Why all the secrecy? Why drag Willie into it at all? I guess I don't understand."

"It sounded like a lot of fun," Jeff began, knowing his words were sounding pretty thin, falling terribly flat. *What can I say?* "She really wanted us to stay up together and watch this movie and just have a party, sort of," he elaborated, "and I just didn't think Mom would let me stay over. I was going to tell Irene no, but when Mom wanted to go out last night too…"

"You think Mom wouldn't let you stay over with this friend of yours?" Lorna mused aloud. "Well, I don't know. It's hard to know what she will or won't do sometimes, but did it ever occur to you to <u>ask</u>?"

"Sure, but then Mom would want to call Irene."

Lorna scratched an ear that itched, then her nose. "I'm afraid I still don't get it. Why would that be so terrible?"

Then, "why Jeff?" Lorna asked again.

Jeff's reply was barely audible. "Because…" Jeff said "when we first met, she thought that I was a girl."

That one took a while to choke down, but then to Lorna, at least, a lot of things started making a lot more sense. Jeff was looking appealingly now at his older sister, who's mouth still hung open in numb surprise, but soon she pulled herself together, shut her mouth and went over to sit on the bed next to Jeff. "Think you wanna tell me about it?" Lorna asked, rather hoping in some ways that he wouldn't.

"At first, I didn't mean to," he said hollowly. "I saw the job and I wanted it, <u>really</u> wanted it. Ms. Larson said I should call her, so I did, and she thought I was a girl and when she asked me what my name was and she was offering me the job, well, I gave a different name…" Jeff/Jennifer trailed off and sat silently.

Very slowly, Lorna nodded. "And because she was blind…" Lorna left the statement unfinished.

"Mmm-hmmm."

"Jeeze," she said. "Things would have gone better if <u>you'd</u> gone to the fashion show, and I'd spent the night with your friend." Then she wished she hadn't said it. "Oh, I'm sorry Jeff. I didn't mean…"

But Jeff held up a hand and there was a sheepish sort of grin on his face- and tears in his eyes. "We didn't do anything wrong," he said. "We just-just like being together." *Liked being together*, he corrected himself mentally.

"I know, Jeff. I don't think anybody would suspect you of doing anything wrong, not like that." But Lorna noted disconcertedly that now, Jeff looked if anything, more miserable than he had when he'd come in. The anger had gone, leaving just that lost kid behind.

"It's just not the same now."

"What isn't?"

"Irene and me," Jeff complained. "She was supposed to be <u>my</u> friend, and now Mom and her are talking and Irene's treating me like a dumb kid, saying that I've got to go home and tell my Mommy what I've been doing, before she calls up and tells her herself, and now they're-well, talking over my head, like I'm not even here."

"How could you know that, Jeff?" Lorna intervened as gently as she could, considering that Jeff was starting to sound like a stuck record.

"Well, why did they have to talk so long anyhow!?" Anger, jealousy and embarrassment mingled suddenly and Jeff bolted from his sister's room and down the hall to slam his own door behind him.

Lorna helplessly watched him go, knowing that she'd said what she could, done what she could do, but not feeling any comfort from the knowing. And this would not be the last time Jeff/Jennifer would feel abandoned, betrayed, affronted in the days to come, for the path s/he had chosen when first borrowing a girl's name and going abroad in her image was a road with neither signposts nor easy footing.

After he'd cooled down a bit, Jeff realized that he (she), had been doing a lot of running and flying off the handle today. Part of him wanted to go apologize at least to Lorna, but Lorna'd know he was sorry. Lorna was okay, considering she was a Big Sister.

Jeff got up from his own bed, picked up the coat he'd flung on the floor when he'd come stalking up here, smarting from the intimacy he'd posited between his mom and Irene. *I wonder what they were talking about.* Almost, he'd eavesdropped longer, but wasn't sure he wanted to hear whatever it was. Jeff wasn't sure if it would be worse for them to be discussing him, or something entirely different-leaving him out altogether. He carried the coat over to his closet and, freeing a hanger to put it on, encountered the green, pink, yellow and brown flowered pattern of the dress Mom had given him-when? Three days ago? Four? *A picture's worth a thousand words,* he thought. *Maybe I should put this on and then just run downstairs, out into the street and all through town. Sure would save a lot of talking.* With her heart still heavy, Jennifer shut the closet door, got a book and settled down to read.

Chapter 8.

A Slight Case of Detection…

The rest of the weekend just sort of dragged by with Jeff still feeling like Mom said he acted sometimes, like a whipped puppy who's just lost his best friend. Well, come to think of it… Still, there was nobody to accuse him because Jeff stayed pretty much to himself Saturday and Sunday. Mom had work to make up Saturday afternoon and part of Sunday, and Lorna-as always she had plenty to do.

I wish I had something to do, something to keep real busy with, that I could do all by myself-or at least not need somebody to do it with!

Like a tangled skein of yarn or a hastily discarded wad of packing string, Jeff followed each strand of this project, this month, this part of his life to the nearest knot, untying that only to find more knots. First, the project, and that was all tangled up with Irene. Then Irene herself, who had wanted a helper and a friend, and Jeff, or Jennifer had been both… And how much effort had gone into bringing Jennifer to life? More like making her real, or something not entirely of the imagination. But now, Irene knew, and so did Lorna to a degree. So, is Jennifer real anymore? Jeff found it was very important that Jennifer be real. But what good would that be? What did either of them have left to do?

Sunday afternoon, when Lorna was off to her science teacher's house with the model and Mom had gone to the office for a couple of hours-("There's casserole in the fridge when you're hungry. Just heat it up.") Jeff hauled himself off his bed and went again to look at the dress. He took it down, holding the print up against him, walking out across the hall to the full-length mirror on the bathroom door. Yes, it would be a little big. Jeff carefully returned the print to his own room, then went and got the blue cotton one, now laundered and ironed again, from Lorna's closet.

Jennifer went downstairs, taking them two at a time in the brown sandals. She peered first out the living room picture-window, then out the window above the kitchen sink. She finally settled on a place in the dining-room where the sliding glass door, with drapes partially closed, provided both privacy and a commanding view of both driveway and street. Jennifer put the somewhat stale percolator of coffee on to heat (having removed and washed the innards thereof), and poured a cup of scalding black coffee which she carried to the dining room table. She set the cup on previously circumscribed rings on a magazine, selected one of Mom's back issues of the Atlantic Monthly and thumbed through poetry and prose, fact and fiction. Coffee was something allowable only on special occasions, but wasn't this one special? Besides, the pot would be cooled off again before Mom got back.

Later, Jennifer carefully returned the dress to it's hanger, observing that she was getting almost as good as Mom at hanging up stuff. "No, I'm not gone away," she declared. (Nor-as it turned out, had the repercussions from the week just past.)

Monday afternoon, on the way to fifth-period Study Hall, Jeff heard "psst!" from one of the nearby doorways and turning to look, saw Willie peering around the door of the A. V. room.

"McGowan! Get <u>in</u> here," Willie hissed. "Dontcha' want yer Mad...?" Willie held out the magazine, partly concealed in a battered Spelling Book.

The Audio-video room, right next to the school library, was empty except for Willie and now Jeff. "Deal's a deal," Willie said, holding out the Mad. "You got me the Coors, I got you the magazine."

Surprised at Willie's jovial demeanor, Jeff took the Mad. "Thanks, Willie. You mean you didn't get in trouble, Friday?"

"No-o-o-o," Willie said, round-eyed with sarcasm, then he grimaced. "Of COURSE I got in trouble!" he said disgustedly, "but so will you. Which reminds me," Willie reached into his pants pocket, "of something else I had for you. You musta' dropped 'em in the locker room when you were putting on your lipstick." With that, Willie drew out the frayed pair of pink panties that had gone missing last Thursday, holding them up in front of Jeff's face. "Always wondered about you, Jeffie. But now I know the reason you were wearing a skirt over at that blind chick's house, is because you're a girl too."

They stared at each other for a few moments, Jeff feeling himself beginning to tremble while Willie's grin widened.

"Well," Willie stretched out the bikinis, expanding the waistband, "what color are you wearing today? Let's have a look. Pull down your pants, why don't ya!" Willie glanced at the door, then back to Jeff. "If the librarian comes in, you can just say you had a rock in your shoe…"

Willie looked sluggish, but was bigger than Jeff and surprisingly fast. Before Jeff could reach the door, Willie moved to block it, fluttering his prize.

In spite of the alarm, Jeff wondered what Jennifer Wright or Susan, or- anybody would think if they walked in seeing Willie and him like this. Willie shut the door.

"You know what I'm going to make you do, McGowan?" The front of Willie's pants was bulging, he shoved his right hand to hover at his zipper while the scrap of pink nylon hung like a breezeless banner from his left. "I mean, since you wanna be a girl and all." Willie made smacking noises with his lips. "Either that… or I could go over to Mr. Munger's office and show him what I found in your locker basket."

Jeff looked around wildly. There was no other door to the A. V. room and there wasn't any way to get Willie away from the one route of escape there was-at least without making a lot of noise and bringing a lot of attention to both of them.

"So," Willie taunted, starting to unzip himself. "What's it gonna be?" *What-else-can-I-do?*

The knob turned and the door swung suddenly inward, nearly knocking Willie off balance. "May I ask what's going on in here?"

Willie's hand opened, allowing the purloined panties to flutter to the floor.

Ms. Larson looked puzzled, then harried. "Good grief, Willie," she said in resigned exasperation. "Aren't you a little young for fraternity pranks?"

"But they're McGowan's!" Willie said earnestly, averting his eyes from the evidence of his mischief.

"Oh, get along with you, Willie!" Ms. Larson said, now in real annoyance.

"No, really," Willie protested. "I found them in the locker room in Gym last Thursday. They were hanging out of McGowan's locker. I was just…" (here Willie looked slyly over at Jeff) "giving them back to him."

"Fine, Willie. Go to Study Hall, please."

Willie lost no time getting out the door and out of sight of the teacher, but when Jeff made as if to follow, Ms. Larson crooked a finger. (Bending down,) "Let's take a walk."

Ms. Larson led the way down the hall to the teacher's lounge, which was currently vacant. She pointed to a chair, seating herself and gazed thoughtfully at Jeff. "Let's just say I heard part of the conversation," she said diplomatically. "Willie's mother called this morning, to ask about his behavior at school. You didn't know that though, since I didn't tell you." She grinned. "Now I find him badgering you in a location where neither of you have any business being. Is there a problem between the two of you?"

"He seems to have it in for me," Jeff said.

"Evidently," she agreed. "But, is this about some particular conflict you boys are having right now, or merely more of the general razzing with which we are all so familiar-those of us who share this school with Willie?"

"Oh, we've been having some problems outside of school," Jeff told her, "a disagreement, sort of."

"But it has started affecting things in school. Right?"

"I guess…"

Ms. Larson took some time choosing what to say next. "Is the nature of this disagreement you and Willie are having" she asked, "something in which your teachers, or perhaps a school counselor should be involved?"

"No," Jeff told her, feeling honest enough in doing that.

"Then is there anything we need to do about keeping you two from-resolving disagreements at school? Possibly referring them to a parent, or staying separated?"

"Okay," Jeff agreed, since teachers took it as an article of faith that any problem could be solved by the expedient of Walking Away…

"All right, then," Ms. Larson said. "Now, regarding the (ahem!) item, found on the A. V. room floor," and Jeff squirmed, "was any of what Willie was saying, ah, true?"

Jeff gulped. "You know Irene?"

"Why, yes." Ms. Larson smiled. "She and I had a lovely talk on Friday. In fact, that's one of the reasons I want to talk with you. What has she to do with any of this?"

"The reason Irene wanted a girl in the first place," Jeff began to explain, "is that she designs clothes and sews a first copy of everything so she can demonstrate her designs."

"Yes," his teacher said. "I believe we've spoken about this. So, you are helping her with this enterprise?"

"You see," Jeff said, "she needed a model for some of her things-and (gulp) a lot of her designs are for women's things."

"O-o-oh…" But Ms. Larson still looked puzzled. "I still have a certain amount of confusion here…"

I guess I've got myself painted into this one, Jeff thought. "Well," he said, "I have to look in a mirror and see if things fit smoothly or not and, you know, boy's underwear just doesn't look right underneath. We're making a dress for my sister," he added, "and that has to do with our Service project too."

"Hmm," said Ms. Larson. "An interesting means of crashing the gender barrier, Mr.? McGowan. So," she exhaled, shrugging in exaggerated unconcern. "So these would appear to be-yours. Might one suggest perhaps greater care in safe-guarding such-private items?"

A moment later she said "is it safe to inquire just what all your Service project involves?"

"It's not all settled yet," Jeff told her, "but it's going to involve Lorna."

"Really?" Ms. Larson asked in surprise. "How so?"

"Lorna's doing her project about helping wheelchair bound people get into the library," Jeff enthused. "Irene is trying to get into a school of clothing design so she can do original stuff, and she's designing special clothes for disabled people. That's one of the things I'm helping her with."

"I must say," his teacher smiled broadly, "you do have an impressive family. I don't mind telling you that when we began this interview I was not just a little bit concerned about your ability to cope in the Seventh Grade arena. Your volunteer experience should ideally lead you into new areas of knowledge and I guess you can't go much further in that direction. -Still, remember something for me won't you?"

"Sure. What?"

"Just that while it's fine to experiment, to explore, it's also important to protect ourselves. Isn't it?"

Jeff nodded.

"Great!" Ms. Larson patted Jeff's shoulder. "You're a remarkable person Mr. McGowan. A bit of a *caution,* as granny would say, but hardly ever dull…"

Walking now, finally to Study Hall, Jeff wondered what it would have been like. What if Ms. Larson hadn't gotten there in time and he'd had to do what Willie wanted? Ms. Larson's advice about protecting yourself certainly made sense, but… Jeff had to admit, the idea had been intriguing, even sort of exciting in a scary sort of way. *Is that what people are going to think about me?* Jeff wondered, *when they find out-that I like to be a girl?* Then the other thought, was everything Willie'd said been based only upon a chance glimpse of Jennifer at Irene's then whatever he might have seen in the bathroom last week? Or had Willie somehow figured things out before? *And now he's been following me around.* A guilty voice asked within-*if it wasn't an accident, no, two accidents, how would Willie have known?*

After the confrontation with Willie Jackson and the subsequent conversation between Jeff and Ms. Larson, the latter returned to her classroom and sat with chin on fist considering her role as a teacher, a human being, and as an 'other than conventional' person. Not always arrayed in that order, for the three aspects tended often to be in conflict.

Elizabeth had briefly considered going to the office after a master key to the lockers, just in case Jeff's secrecy was causing him to plumb dangerous depths, whatever they might turn out to be. She'd rejected the idea though, partly because in order to search a locker she might need to reveal more of what she already knew than she was willing. *Though I don't know much.*

Her relationship with Jeff was supposed to be one of trust, wasn't it? *And even though we weren't supposed to be friends, per se, with the students--* Elizabeth argued, *--we can at least try to be benevolant mentors, and, I like the kid!* As a teacher of course, and as a professional, Elizabeth had a responsibility to her school, her principal, the school board for that matter, and to herself, to bring to light any sort of behavior of a dangerous or proscribed nature. But, as a Lesbian, she was all too aware of how easily an effort to assist could turn into stigmatizing or worse.

What would I rather the teacher who found out about Julia and me being- a Couple had done, instead of what did happen? That had been Elizabeth's Sophomore year in High School, and while she now knew that the teacher's choices were limited (*are limited*), it was one thing to merely follow policy in a given situation. It was quite another to become the policing agent which decided which policy it was that must be followed. Still, leaving well enough alone wasn't really an option either.

She consulted her teacher's directory, hung poised for several long breaths, the point of a #2 black lead pencil darkening the spot… "Alice

McGowan please. Yes, Mrs. McGowan, this is Elizabeth Larson, Jeff's roll room teacher." The conversation began with the usual nervous civilities which take place in an unscheduled teacher to parent communique, the purpose of which is still apt to be negative. "What I needed to ask, Alice," said Elizabeth, "is whether you've noticed any recent change in Jeff's attitude about-school? Or perhaps any of his classmates?"

(Somewhat defensively,) "I work, as you doubtless know, since you've called me at the Office," Alice told her. "I can say though that Jeff's been busier than is usual," she laughed self-consciously. "I forget what a great help the boy is around the house until he's gone," she said.

"Gone, with his Special Friend?" Ms. Larson prompted.

"Irene? The blind woman? Yes, a delightful person. I'm glad Jeff's found something in which he can take such an interest-frankly," Jeff's mother countered.

Ms. Larson plunged again. "It seems a good thing then that Jeff spends so much time with a woman more than twice his age?" She said it like a statement not a question.

"It's his project," Jeff's mother told her with labored patience.

"I'm afraid we had a little incident at school today," Ms. Larson reported. "Nothing all that unusual among young boys, unfortunately, but another student, Willie Jackson seemed to be harassing Jeff
about something that was evidently in his locker."

"The Jackson boy? Oh yes, they had an agreement to spend the night together Friday, and Jeff ended by not going. Some falling out evidently, possibly concerning some of the boys drinking. I'd imagine the incident stemmed from that---something in Jeff's locker?"

"Alice, is there any reason why Jeff would be keeping girl's clothes at school?"

"Oh yes!" Mrs. McGowan chuckled with hearty relief. "He's making a birthday dress for his older sister. Irene sews, which I think is entirely amazing! So Jeff was bringing something over to Irene's house to use as a pattern."

"Is there a reason he would need to bring his sister's underclothes as well?"

"Whew!" Alice McGowan laughed again. "Who knows what goes through kid's minds. Things were a lot simpler" (she sighed) "when I was a girl. No, I don't know any reason for Jeff to have his sister's underclothes. I generally keep up with the laundry, but kids experiment don't they? Who knows."

The conversation having reached stalemate, "I just thought we should talk," said Ms. Larson somewhat weakly. "Please don't get me wrong. Jeff is an excellent student, and we are very proud of him. I only wondered if we could both be just a little more involved in his project... It's a pretty ambitious one when you think of it,"

"As I'm sure you know," said Jeff's mother "it isn't easy for a mother trying to raise a son alone. I'd put him in scouts, or a boy's club, but Jeff is so studious and sort of aloof, I don't really want to force him. I tell you what Elizabeth, we're having Irene over for dinner Wednesday. Would you consider joining us?"

(Tangled strings.) Jeff had not been denied permission to call or visit Irene, but neither had he asked. Sure it had been a blow to his self-esteem to be obligated, under a certain amount of duress to inform his mother of the thing he'd gone to so much trouble to conceal, that was true- but the experience had served more than anything else to emphasize the difference in their ages, Irene's and his own.

Directly off the hall was a room made up vaguely to resemble a sort of combination sitting and dining room, dominated by a table with white cloth, a vase of somewhat wilted flowers, and copies of Redbook, Good Housekeeping and Ladies' Home Journal. The complex seemed to be deserted. Jeff ventured further into the cluster of rooms, passing multi kitchenettes, sewing machine room, and pantry. Near the back through there was a little cubicle office and there, on her grading period just now, was the Home Economics teacher.

She looked up from a stack of Foods Tests. "Good heavens. You scared me. What may I do for you, young gentleman?"

Miss Jensen was nearing retirement. She wore neatness and decorum like some foreign language teachers wear an acquired accent.

"My name is Jeff," Jeff said, not because that was particularly relevant, but because it seemed the proper thing to do. "I was just wondering..."

"Yes?" Miss Jensen's whitening bun bobbed in a nod of encouragement.

Though Jeff had rehearsed what he'd need to say a dozen times, the words were refusing to come out in an orderly way. "I'm helping a blind lady," he said, "and she sews."

"Admirable." Miss Jensen bobbed again. "Yes?"

"Um, she was helping me make a dress for my sister's birthday? But she's going to school too and she might not have time to work with me."

"That's too bad?"

"I don't know if…" Jeff rushed through the rest of it, "if maybe I could use one of the sewing machines here at school. In here?" he added, in case it might be suspected that he thought sewing machines might exist elsewhere in the building, "so I can get it done in time?"

To Jeff's immense relief, Miss Jensen laughed, a dry little laugh, but not unkind. "We had the Bachelor's Cooking Class in the fall," she told him. "I don't recall having a young man in the sewing room before. Some of the ladies come in Fifth Period to use the machines. I guess there wouldn't be anything wrong if you wanted to do that…"

Then she plied Jeff with a string of rapid-fire questions about darts, pleats or lack of pleats, tucks, trims, gussets, smocking, styles-hardly waiting for answers, not needing to listen long when she did stop.

"I'm not sure."

"Well then," she said, "let me know when you have a better idea of what you want to do. Fair enough?"

"Fair enough." Jeff nodded back. "Thank you."

Jeff made straight for the Public Library, was disconcerted to find Jennifer not on duty today, but located the elderly assistant librarian shelving newly-arrived periodicals. "I need to find some books on sewing. Dress-making, for a school project," he told her. *Well, why not. I'm a girl, aren't I?*

With three books under his arm, Jeff turned toward home. It would be the easiest thing to bend his path toward Irene's, go on like nothing had changed. There was much he longed to discuss with his friend, things of a scary, embarrassing, fascinating, and very private nature. Everywhere he turned it seemed that Irene's name came up, even trying to work apart from Irene in order to fulfil the obligation to his mother he'd rashly made, he must invoke Irene's name. Community Awareness Month would be over at the end of the month, just a little over two weeks away, and at the end of that, Miss Larson would be expecting a presentation from both of them.

"How did things get so complicated?" Jeff inquired, of an errant crow pecking a piece of moldy bread near the curbing. "I started out just <u>reading</u> and being friends." For Jeff, for Jennifer, Irene was Community Awareness Month and, deadline or not, neither of them was ready to go back there. *I've just got to have more time to figure things out-to untie the knots.*

Chapter 9.

A Decent Proposal: and-
Some Children's Stories

Wednesday afternoon, when school was over, Jeff sat with his chin on his hands in the public library, back in Literature where Lorna never went, making no pretense whatever of reading the sewing primer lying in front of him.

"Hello, Jeffrey."

Nearly jumping off his chair, Jeff swiveled about.

"Jennifer…" The girl whose name it was that first leapt to mind when Irene had asked him to identify himself. Now he felt unaccountably guilty about using it like that. But her smile was bright, cheerful.

"Hi Jeff-how does the dress fit?"

"What!?"

She giggled merrily. "Aren't you supposed to be making a dress for your sister?"

"Oh, yeah, that-I'm going to, but it's barely started yet," Jeff told her, relieved that answering was so easy.

"Well," she laughed, "did we hear about you!"

"Really?" (alarm once more.)

"Oh yes. Miss Jensen was chewing everybody out in home-ec today. Some of the girls really messed up their projects, and we're all supposed to make a dress. Anyhow, Miss Jensen told us that if 'that Jeff McGowan boy' could make a new party dress for his sister, and teach a blind lady to sew besides, we could learn too! She almost swore!" Jennifer Wright finished delightedly.

Jeff sat stunned for a minute, then began laughing along with her. "Oh heck," he said eventually, "has she got things backward."

"You do sew though?" she asked, a little suspiciously, when Jeff had sketched out the less interesting aspects of his friendship with Irene.

"I'm learning," he admitted. "I can run a pretty straight seam, and I've helped with pattern-making, but if anybody's doing the teaching, it's not me."

"Join the club then." Jennifer smiled. "Woman's work is never done, they say, and I'm going to be about another year or two on my project-Who'd have known?"

"Known what?"

"Oh, when we saw that announcement last month and we were all choosing our assignments, everyone just assumed that a blind lady would want somebody to help her. I don't think anyone imagined that it would be *her* who would do the helping."

It's not quite like that--! Aloud, Jeff said "speaking of assignments, how's your project coming along?"

"Oh, Mrs. Pemberton isn't all that bad, as long as books come in on time, and about a million other things, but I'm learning a lot." Jennifer looked at the clock on the library wall. "I guess Susan is a bit critical sometimes."

As if on cue, Susan Manchester walked through the library door. "Oh, hi Jeff," she said in a stage whisper when she was still two dozen feet from the back table.

"I'd better go." Jennifer moved to join her friend.

Lagging behind the two girls, now engaged in animated talk, Jennifer's words came back to him, and momentarily, his irritation. (Who'd have imagined that it would be Irene who would do the helping.) It was funny in a way. Irene and him, Irene and her, they needed each other. They ALL did. Why then couldn't they all recognize that?

She hasn't called me either. She could have asked me to come over and read, or do Math or anything.

Couldn't you have made up some reason to go see her-to check on her or something?

I was scared, Jennifer admitted, as Susan and the other Jennifer turned a corner out of sight. *I am scared.*

A sheath dress, Jeff decided. It would be simple to make-compared to most of the alternatives-and Lorna, tall and slender, would look smart in it. Thinking of the next interview with Miss Jensen, he suddenly felt very disloyal, not only to Irene, but even to Gussie, Irene's Sears sewing machine. "I'm sorry…" but there was nobody to hear, not even a crow, not even a mirror to lock eyes with. And the leaden weight had increased with a gravid stridency.

Alice McGowan had come home early to start dinner for her guests, but in her fairly haphazard way of getting things done around home (or not), she'd neglected to tell Jeff that he should expect company this evening. So when Jeff walked in at twenty after five, to see Irene fidgeting on the couch, looking apprehensive and out of place-as Jeff felt sometimes, it was all he could do not to whoop and throw himself on his friend. Irene had been (furtively to begin with) probing her own feelings about the project she and Jeff had outlined on that ill-fated Friday, Elizabeth being recently added to her internal discussion.

"Howdy, stranger," Irene said, turning her face toward Jeff. "Thought you were getting kept in after school or something!"

"We let him out," said Ms. Larson, who had been deep in conversation with Lorna, "just this once, for good behavior. Right, Jeff?" Elizabeth read the look of apprehension on her pupil's face.

Irene, also feeling the tension, said "look out Jeff, they're cutting out more work for us!"

Mom intervened with dinner before discomfort or misunderstanding could crystallize and grow.

Alice McGowan had seated her daughter and Jeff's teacher on her own left and right, setting the two places across the table for Jeff and his friend. "You can help Irene," she said aside to her son, "since you know what sorts of things she likes to eat."

"Oh," said Jeff, "she helps herself pretty well."

"I've already sliced the roast." Alice directed this to the blind woman. "I hope you like roast beef?"

"Sure do. Just toss a hunk this direction. I'll do the rest."

"I've been talking with your sister, Jeff" said Elizabeth Larson, deflecting the conversation away from the feeding of blind people, "and I'm fascinated by the areas of overlap between what she is doing and the project you and Irene are developing."

Jeff said nothing, sensing that his teacher's comments were directed more at his sister than at him. For her own part, Lorna was hoping devoutly that this would not turn out to be still another of her mother's schemes to get her to behave in a more acceptable feminine manner.

"I'm an alternative energy specialist, basically," Lorna announced, bristling just a little, "but the emphasis is on alternative."

"So I surmised," Elizabeth agreed. "And the more I speak with Irene here, and with Jeff, the more I'm struck by the truly alternative (and original) nature of their own project. This leads me to propose what will probably sound like the most radical idea of all."

All eyes were now on the teacher.

"Yeah?" said Jeff, uneasily.

"I'm going to propose," Elizabeth Larson continued, "to ask-to explore! that you consider letting Willie Jackson onto your project."

"Willie!" Jeff cried in horror. "Willie hates my guts."

"I wonder," his teacher said. "He does seem to follow you around a great deal, and take a lot of interest in what you are doing. I rather think that deep down, Willie admires you."

"Admires me?" Jeff couldn't believe what he was hearing. "Willie makes my life miserable. He takes every chance he can to give me a bad time!"

"True," Elizabeth interjected smoothly, "but I think you'd find that people who spend their time being annoying or disruptive to others, usually do that because they're dissatisfied with themselves or just haven't found anything better…" She paused to let this sink in, then added "I can tell you that Willie has been on three different projects, and has lasted no more than a couple of days on each. Still, he seems to be very interested in yours, so shall we just say that I'd take it very kindly if you, and Irene, would consent to give Willie a chance to participate."

Irene swallowed a mouthful of buttered potato and turned toward Jeff. "Whaddya' say, Pard? Do we let 'im in?"

"I-don't-know," Jeff said. Although it *was* something to have Willie need something from him, or Ms Larson thought so. "What does Willie think about it?"

"Who's idea do you think it was in the first place?" his teacher replied blandly.

"I'm not at liberty to discuss details at this time," put in Irene, "some of which are highly classified (meaning we haven't yet approached Lorna), but it occurs to me that some of the-mechanical tasks associated with one or both projects-might provide an excellent opportunity for young Willie's talents to-shine."

"I've got just the place for Willie," Lorna offered, half-jokingly. "After all, something might go wrong!" She grinned over at her little brother. "Don't worry about Willie, kid," she said. "I'll put him to work."

Leaning over, "Willie Jackson thinks a training bra has wheels on it," Irene whispered.

Jeff grinned across at his sister, feeling warmer than he had for a while.

"So does Lorna," he whispered back.

Alice McGowan had begun the meal thinking that her scheme to get everyone together was destined to flop miserably. The way Jeff's previously sullen face had just lighted up though, was all the vindication she needed.

Jeff got up to help his mother in clearing the table before dessert was served. When they were alone in the kitchen, Alice said (squirting canned topping on bakery shortcakes and thawed, sliced strawberries), "now that we are all busy agreeing, I'm going to agree with your sister to pick you up some new underwear the first chance she gets, so that you will not find it necessary to borrow a Larger Size." The private smile she gave Jeff's teacher as Alice set the dessert glass in front of her contained more than a little self-satisfaction.

"Good to have you back," Jeff murmured, as he slid back into the chair next to Irene.

Irene lightly fisted Jeff's arm. "I was never anyplace else (she dropped her voice), Jen."

The house had emptied and Alice stood alone in her kitchen, transferring dishes from soapy to rinse then putting the roast platter in to soak. How long had it been since she'd had a housefull for dinner? Too long, probably, she guessed. When she and James had moved from L. A. to settle in this little community, not fifty miles from the Canadian border, they had found this fine, big house, newly built-how different things were supposed to have been!

During the building boom of the '50s, James' architectural practice had taken off like the proverbial rocket and, waiting to get pregnant, Alice had taken a part time accounting job. The McGowans had slipped easily into the rounds of dinner parties and other social events of young and coming professionals and professional wives. When Lorna had come, then Jeff, they seemed to have achieved the Hugh Beaumont-Barbara Billingsly sort of life that was almost the only sort allowable on the cumbersome black and white TV of the time. Then had come the heart attack.

Alice had gone to night school to complete her CPA certification. Her part time job expanded to fill her days-*and there went my vision of afternoon tennis and garden tea parties.* The kids had never truly wanted for anything, not really, except for time, Alice admitted for the umpteenth time with genuine regret. *But, at least they're a pair of scholars. They have that from both of us-Jim.* She took a fresh dish-towel from the drawer, dabbed a tear with one corner, then began wiping the shamrock-pattern guest china. In the hawthorn out back, a late-roosting robin sang in the twilight.

Elizabeth Larson gave Irene a lift home and came in to have a look at some of her work. Her ulterior motive didn't take long to surface.

"I design."

"Oh, I thought this was a hobby."

"I'm making up coursework to prepare for the technical college program in textile and clothing design."

"Is this a longtime interest of yours?"

"Quite long," Irene told her. "Making up coursework by correspondence takes a while and there's the matter of being taken seriously."

Suddenly, Elizabeth Larson could see what Irene and Jeff might well have in common. *Yes, I wish there was an Irene for me when I was twelve,* she thought. "So your contribution to our spring program is a genuine display of invention, prototypes?"

"You could say that," Irene said, nettled a little by the note of surprise in the teacher's voice, the unconscious hint of condescension.

"This is fascinating!" Elizabeth Larson adopted, for the first time, a genuine tone with her, as far as Irene was concerned. "Wish we had this in high school." She studied the garments arrayed on Irene's kitchen table. "A bit of a reach though, for Jeff to tell me that your project requires him to come to work in lingerie?"

"No requirement from my project..." Irene replied.

"Meaning?"

"Meaning, that he's taken quite a stand, but he respects my individuality, I respect his, hers. So far as I'm concerned that's the end of it."

"That's ridiculous," Ms. Larson expostulated. "Twelve-year old boys don't go around in their sister's clothes. What did you think you were doing, abetting such behavior?"

"I'm blind, remember?" Irene returned innocently. "Jeff, Jennifer's voice sounded girlish enough to me. I don't ask for credentials."

Ms. Larson fumed, twisting and untwisting a handkerchief she'd impulsively pulled from her purse.

"Let me tell you a story," Irene said. "When I was in the State School..."

"Well," --carefully Irene marshaled her thoughts. "In a boarding school, at least the one I was in, the teachers and house-parents have more or less the power of life and limb, or at least the ability to make your life miserable, let's say. Charlie was a kid about my age. He was about the sweetest boy I knew, which means that unlike other boys his age, he didn't live to make things rough on any girl he met. At this school there was a chapter of Campfires, back before Campfires were co-ed, for the blind girls. There wasn't any Boy Scout troop and the activities for boys there were always supervised by the sports coach who was-a pain. When we were about eleven, Charlie decided that he wanted to join the Campfires.

At first the gym teachers at the school used a lot of hazing and general bullying to shame Charlie out of this 'sissy stuff' you know, extra laps in gym till he dropped and trips through the paddle line if he was late for P. E. class. Charlie didn't come through it like John Wayne exactly, but he kept showing up at meetings, and he really fit in okay. We girls thought it was a lark to make the authorities all pissed, so we accepted him.

Then, the school tried another tack. They tried to shame Charlie out of it. They called him Charlene and stopped taking him to the barber. Finally they made him wear dresses to class. Charlie just said that he was a real Campfire girl like everybody else, and it didn't seem to bother him. One day somebody remembered that Charlie had been in dresses for weeks now, and he seemed to be going on like business as usual. Even the boys had gotten tired of making fun of Charlie, but the faculty was bughouse."

Irene paused here.

"What happened then?" Elizabeth demanded, intrigued in spite of herself.

"Sad about that," Irene said, her head a little lowered.

"When nothing seemed to work, the school decided to pretend nothing had ever happened. All punishments were removed. Later they ordered Charlie to stop coming to school in girls' clothes. He wasn't acting in a sufficiently masculine manner, you see. We were the only people he trusted at all. Charlie's grades fell from B-plus to Ds and Es. He was despondent. He ran away from school three times. I haven't seen him since."

"He ran away?! He was blind?"

"Oh, he wasn't all by himself," Irene said. "There's nothing to prevent blind kids running away really, if there's somebody to go with. It's probably a bit easier for them to be preyed upon than somebody who can run away from a specific person rather than a general situation..." Irene was quiet for a moment. "It just seems to me," she said, "that if people would leave well enough alone, Charlie'd have avoided an awful lot of misery. All he wanted was to spend some of his time with the people he thought he belonged with."

"That's <u>inappropriate</u>," Elizabeth said reflexively. "Of course the school authorities had to do something, though their methods might be suspect."

"What's inappropriate? The fact that Charlie wanted to play with girls? You're a teacher. Is it inappropriate for us to raise boys to denigrate and shame girls and women? Sometimes it's kind of refreshing to find the exception."

"I'm sorry," Irene said at length. "A school system that was supposed to offer every child a good education, which left me years behind in math and several other subjects so at the age of 27 I'm still struggling to go to a two year college-the way people act shocked that I even know how to dress myself-I guess maybe you see things a little differently if you have never known what it's like to be like everybody else."

Elizabeth Larson sat quietly, examining a series of rebuttals, rejecting each. "I know," she said finally.

For a time the two women sat quietly, Elizabeth studying the mousy brown hair, the unremarkable face with it's stubby, somewhat upturned nose, the pale, green eyes-which though unseeing, seemed to view the world with such a note of irreverent mischief. *Still...* she inwardly affirmed, *...it would have been nice if there'd been an Irene-back then.*

"I wouldn't have you think," Elizabeth winced at the hint of conciliation in her voice, "that it's all been roses for me either." Irene continued to sit impassive, a nervous blinking of the eyes and an automatic smile betraying the fact that she had heard.

Though it had been the farthest thing from her mind when they'd arrived, Elizabeth found herself talking on-not about her student or Irene, but about Elizabeth Larson, frightened fifteen-year-old, and the troubling discovery of her own-Difference. "I don't know what tipped them off," she paused to check the turmoil that resurfaced even after all these years. "Somebody remarked one day that our <u>eyes</u> looked alike. That's all she said, but we freaked." Elizabeth considered. "You may not know this," she explained hastily, "but people's eyes, when they're in love, come to look like each other-<u>alike</u> I mean-or at least that's what people think."

Heavenly day, Irene remarked sub voce, *what if somebody with 20/20 vision fell madly in love with somebody born totally without--!*

"Like I said," Elizabeth told her, as if she'd heard the interruption. "We panicked, and probably started acting weird as hell. I don't know. Before either of us knew what was happening though, it was all over the school. Teachers got involved-the principal-parents." The sense of utter shame, of being dirtied by other people's lies-their fears came flooding back.

"It ended up," she concluded the sad narrative, "that Julie's parents sent her East to a boarding school while I stayed to face the music. Nobody really had anything on us, so I still graduated and even got into the University without any problem, but I tell you-it felt pretty creepy around the old high school for a while-until the other kids found something else to make a sensation over."

"Yes," Irene nodded. "I can well imagine."

(Again that quizzical little smirk on the blind woman's face!) "But we really weren't doing anything," Elizabeth protested with more heat than she'd intended. "We kissed, maybe. Girls do that all the time, but never in public."

Irene said simply "either have we."

"But if one of us had been a boy," Elizabeth nerved herself for one final attempt, "no one would have even questioned."

Irene forbore to give the obvious reply, merely allowing more teeth in the grin. *But Charlie wasn't a girl*, she wanted to rage. *And either is Jeff McGowan!* "Like I said," Irene answered finally. "Sometimes it's better if people just leave well enough alone."

Seeing that there was no possible point to continuing the discussion, Elizabeth rose, taking wary leave of this serenely stubborn woman, no more than two years younger than herself but whose handicap had allowed her to live so oblivious to the outside world.

Elizabeth drove toward home and a long night of philosophical arm-wrestling with herself. As she passed the McGowan's block she spied Jeff deeply engaged in conversation with his tall, severely-attractive sister. Heading toward the projects where she knew Willie's family lived, she honked. *At least I did one thing right today-I think.*

As Lorna and Jeff approached the Jackson's residence, they were startled to find a police car parked in the driveway. *Well, not really surprised*, Jeff thought to himself. Perhaps startled was a better word, startled by this tangible evidence of Willie's delinquency, or that of someone in the household...

"Come here quick." It was Mrs. Jackson, wringing her hands and bearing down on Jeff and Lorna. "Can you tell us anything about last Friday night?"

"Excuse me." The uniformed officer was standing on the porch, beckoning curtly. "Do you kids know anything about this?"

"About what?" Lorna demanded.

"Do you have any idea of Willie's whereabouts Friday evening, between ten-thirty and eleven P.M.?" The policeman looked at Lorna, then at Jeff, then back.

"They're saying Willie set a fire!" Mrs. Jackson wailed.

Jeff thought for a moment, checked the schedule in his mind. "That was when the movie was ending," he announced.

"The what?" The officer looked nonplussed.

"Well, I saw Willie at about that time. You see, the movie ended at eleven and right before then, Willie and the other guys showed up…"

"Was this in a theater, son?"

"No. A friend's house."

"Anybody to vouch for your story? An adult maybe?"

"Yes, and yes officer."

"Why was Willie out at such a late hour?"

"He came to bring me a magazine."

"A what?"

Jeff willed a blush. "A magazine," he said again. "A Mad magazine."

The cop snorted. "You and this Willie good friends, son?"

Jeff's mouth was too dry to open just now. He nodded.

Nobody brought up the subject of the six-pack. The policeman put away his clipboard, saying he'd be in touch if there were any more questions.

"They always blame everything on my Willie," Mrs. Jackson lamented, as the police car disappeared around the corner.

She stood a moment longer on the door-step as if wondering What On Earth to do next, then Mrs. Jackson whined. "I don't know where Willie is… You're looking for him?"

Before either of them could answer, she said again "I don't know where he is," and closed the door, leaving Jeff and Lorna standing in the gravel-strewn street. They were turning to go when Jeff heard a noise, a rustling in the unkempt bushes which choked one side of the duplex's front yard.

Willie's head appeared amongst the foliage, small eyes staring suspiciously at the McGowan kids. "So-" Willy said, "how come didn't ya' squeal on me?"

Jeff cleared his throat. "You didn't set any fires. Did you?"

"Maybe-"

"C'mere, snot," Lorna told him, taking a stride herself toward Willie's hiding place.

Willie crept out of the bushes, but stood as if ready to spring if Lorna got too close, his eyes now surprisingly wide. "Whadda' you want?"

"Just to talk," Lorna said easily. "I've been hearing that you're a guy who can do a pretty good job-in the right place."

"ME!?" Willie said, astonished. "Who told ya' that?"

"A little bird." Lorna stared back, holding the kid's gaze. "It so happens, I've got a job for you, Willie Jackson."

"Yeah? Doing what?"

"I'm building some stuff," she told him. "I need somebody to hold nails while I hammer, find things that get lost, climb up things to see if they fall down- stuff like that."

Willie cracked a grin, which Lorna returned. "I hear you have a lot of experience around school-having been in a bunch of different projects, you pretty much know your way around."

"Well," Willie's chest swelled somewhat. "I guess maybe I do." The next moment, he looked crestfallen once more. "What if I don't know how to do the stuff you want me to?"

"Don't worry," Lorna told him. "You'll be alright. And...(now she put on something between a Russian and an East German accent) ...Eef you dondt, zen you can be ree-edjucatit unt-til you do."

"Well okay then." Willie put out his hand. "It's a deal. Shake."

Lorna shook, then said "right after school tomorrow, squirt. At the library. Don't be late or I'll sock ya'!"

Willie gave Jeff a look as if to say (you have to live with her?) and began making his way, not so rapidly, toward his porch.

"Think he'll show up?" Jeff asked, when they were alone once more and heading toward home.

"He'd better," his sister said, unconcernedly. "Or I'll run him down and drag him there!"

(But for one member-the Special Needs, Community Service Month, Work Committee was emerging: in it's final form.)

Chapter 10.

Pyrotechnics and Private-(Eyes)

Around ten of the Saturday following the dinner party, Alice looked up from her perusal of the financial section of a news-stand New York Times (stocked primarily for herself, she suspected), to notice her son fidgeting as if wanting to be off, yet anxious about testing the routine-ness that had returned to the McGowan home.

"Why don't you get Irene?" she suggested. "And bring her over here for a while. The walk would probably do her a lot of good." Having orchestrated the meeting and eating together of Elizabeth Larson, Irene Carrol, and her own strong-willed children, Alice wished to maintain the initiative she'd thereby gained. Pursuant to this was to encourage some, at least, of Jeff's activities to be closer to home where she could at least maintain a degree of supervision.

"I don't suppose she gets out much," Alice added, as if Irene's exercise were really the cause of her suggestion.

Glad of any errand, Jeff stood, stretched, went to the hall closet for his coat. *He could have called*, his mother thought, as he disappeared out the door. But then, it might more likely get the blind woman out of her abode to simply show up and take her in tow.

Jeff pushed through the lowering grayness of a morning which hadn't decided whether it was really spring, or still lingering winter. He broke into a half-run the last two blocks to Irene's as the mail truck overtook him, and followed the vehicle, as it happened, to the house in question. The deliveryman climbed out of his truck with a flat package in his hand, mounted Irene's porch, slipping a couple of envelopes in the mailbox by Irene's door, then put the package inside the patched screen door. Jeff hung back to let the man get back behind the wheel and drive on, then went up and knocked. "Mail delivery!" he called, as the truck rumbled away.

Irene opened the door in a well-used looking, fuzzy, yellow house-coat with (presumably) the same green nightie Jennifer had borrowed, showing where the robe didn't quite reach in front. "Hi?" she said, "that's you, isn't it?"

Jeff picked up her package and put it into her hand. "It's me."

"Usually my Mom is the only person who comes this early on a Saturday," she told him. "Where's this package from?"

"American Printing House for the Blind," Jeff read.

"My abacus!" Irene stepped back from the door. "Come on in. When I heard you calling out there, I thought you might be a Campfire Girl trying to sell me some mints." Irene grinned mischievously. "No, I guess you'd be about ready for Horizons... How old are you now?"

"Almost thirteen," Jeff told her, as Irene parked herself on the end of the couch and began tearing at the stapled cardboard.

"I'm supposed to Come Get you," Jeff said a few minutes later.

"Yeah?" Who says...?"

"Mom just wanted me out of her hair I guess, but she thought you might like to come over and maybe read and have lunch or something."

"Speaking of reading," Irene snapped her fingers at the sudden recollection, "did young Willie ever give us the magazine we both sacrificed ourselves to get?"

"He did!" Jeff declared. The Monday of the session in the A. V. room, followed by the talk with his teacher, Jeff had been in such a mood to conceal the further proof of his own malcontentcy in his bottom drawer and there it had lain, forgotten. "Yeah, he did give it to me," he said, "but it's at my place."

"Well, let's go there."

Irene set down the abacus, now removed from it's layers of wrapping, and headed for her bedroom, leaving the door open sufficiently to be heard around it. "There's a package of cinnamon rolls on the counter in the kitchen. Help yourself."

Jeff picked up the little device, perhaps six inches by three. It had twelve columns of little buttons (or beads, he supposed). They were arranged so they could slide up and down on a framework of wires. Each column had six beads in it, and there was a bar going across the abacus so that the top bead in each column was separated from the other five. While he was still examining it, Irene reappeared in a pair of jeans and a red pullover, shrugging into a parka.

"How do you like my new toy?" she inquired, as Jeff continued to click-click the little buttons. She helped herself to a roll, took her cane from a corner of the living room. Biting off perhaps a quarter of the former, she tucked the latter under her right arm, holding out her left hand. "Ready to go?"

Jeff returned the fascinating little device to her. "You got some other mail, too," he told her.

Irene flipped open her mailbox, extracting the two transparent-windowed envelopes lurking there. "Bills," she said.

"You want me to read them to you?"

"No, I know what they say. We Want Dough!" She tucked them back into the box.

Holding Jeff's elbow, she stepped lightly off her porch and across the yard with which, garbage or no, her feet were well-accustomed. By the time they reached the road out front, the last bit of the cinnamon roll was stuffed in safely and Irene brought out the cane, holding it diagonally just ahead of her, it's tip barely grazing the ground, should either of them fail to anticipate a curb or break in sidewalk or road. *It's nice to get out someplace different once in a while,* Irene thought. *You learn an area and tend to stick to it.*

"Do you live far from the school, Jen?" Irene asked without thinking.

Her friend darted a glance about to see if anyone was near enough to hear. "Oh, about eight blocks," Jeff/Jen said. "If the distance from my house to the school would be X plus…"

Irene fisted Jeff in the ribs.

Feeling her companion's elbow ascend as Jeff started up to his own front door, Irene adjusted her own stride, and using the cane to catch each riser as it presented, followed up the twelve-step flight with a rapidity which would have horrified Jeff's mother, or probably her own. Mrs. Carroll had never gotten used to her daughter 'just wandering out there in the middle of nowhere--.'

Alice McGowan laid aside the Times as she heard the double set of foot treads on the porch. She rose to greet the visitor and show her to a sitting place but before she could do so, Jeff swung Irene (stalk hanging on to his elbow), so she backed into an arm-chair.

"Kerplunk," he said.

"Good grief, Jeffrey!"

Grinning, Irene shucked her coat and settled down into the venerable seat. "Nice of you to have me over," she said, carefully sliding her cane out of the lane of traffic, alongside her chair.

"Have you heard anything from the college?" Alice asked.

"I've got an interview with the program director next week," Irene told her.

"How are you going to get there?" The words had just slipped out. "-I mean, you're not able to walk all that way?"

"Well, I probably wouldn't try it. I'll probably start out before it's daylight and drive <u>real slow</u>." When Alice didn't laugh, "not real funny," Irene chuckled. "No, it's school related. I'll grab a taxi." Idly, she pushed the abacus from her coat which lay folded on her lap, and began twirling the wheel-like beads.

"That's an abacus, isn't it?" Alice came over to have a closer look. "I saw some of those at the World's Fair back when Lorna was in second grade, and I've always wondered how they work."

"This single bead," Irene showed her, "is a five. These other beads below the crossbar are ones. You move beads toward the crossbar to make the number you want. You can represent any number from one to ten, or zero also, if you push the five up, the ones down, so nothing's next to the crossbar."

"And you can add, subtract, multiply and divide on this," Alice said wonderingly, her accountant's affinity for numbers roused at the improbable-seeming prospect.

"Even take square roots and do fractions," Irene replied, "though I'm not that far yet."

"And you actually work out an answer, like I would with pencil and paper? I mean, it isn't simply a matter of counting beads?"

"That's right." Irene nodded. "I can arrive at an answer just like if I was using my Braille writer or any other device for doing math. And, all in all, I'd say that it's a lot smaller than anything else I've heard of for working problems."

"Hmm," Alice mused. "I was reading the other day that we'll soon have little computers that can fit in your pocket or purse, that will do what one of the big calculators in our office at work can, and they'll only a few hundred dollars!"

"That would be something." Jeff, somewhat miffed at being left out of the discussion, broke in now. "Maybe there'd be a way to make one of those-pocket computers give answers in Braille, or maybe even <u>talk</u> like a Chatty Cathy record."

His mother smiled indulgently. "Yes, nice," she agreed, "but being realistic, something like that would always be too impractical, I'm quite sure."

Jeff decided to file away the idea as something about which to ask Lorna. "Well," he announced, "we've got some studying to do--."

"Fine," his mother said. "I'll call you in a half hour or so for lunch."

"We'll take a right at the top of these stairs," Jeff told Irene, as they trumped up the flight to the second floor. (Don't bother counting stairs,) she'd told Jeff once, (just as long as I know if they're up or down.) "If we turned left, Lorna's room would be at the end of the hall that way," Jeff elaborated now. "Right across from the top of the stairs here is Mom's room, and next to us kind of across from Mom's room is the bathroom. There's a linen closet on the other side of the stairs to our left, and over here to the right, at the other end of this hall, is my room." He led them into the latter and pulled out his desk chair for Irene.

Alice took the still-rolled local paper from the coffee table, and opened it to the front page.

Police Apprehend Suspects
In Sports-Field Conflagration

Below the headline the lead paragraph read;

Sheriff's Deputies announced Friday, that three boys ranging in age from 13 to 15 are being questioned as to their possible role in a fire and series of explosions at the Central Stadium near City Hall, on the Thirteenth.

The article went on to describe how a group of youngsters had begun a bonfire around ten on the Friday of Jeff's Stay-over and had evidently been tossing empty deodorant and hairspray cans into the fire, in order to cause them to explode. A fully, or partially full can of acrylic spray paint had resulted in the fire burning out of control and scorching the grass near the bleachers of the park stadium. Alice scanned down the article for names and was relieved that Willie Jackson's was not among them. This must be what Jeff and Lorna had come home talking about after going over to the Projects that evening, to invite Willie to work with them.

A spokesman for the Mayor's Office (the article ended dolefully), called the event "one more indication of the breakdown in civic conscience-no longer confined to the larger cities in America."

Yes. Alice put down the newspaper. Between the Jackson kids drinking that night, and the fire, in which (thank heaven) Willie had not been involved, evidently, and Jeff's poor choice in an overnight companion (*and my own poor judgement, admit it--*) and teachers getting in a dither! It must have been a full moon as well!

Maybe I should have paid Irene for looking after Jeff, Alice considered. I'd probably have called one of the daughters of somebody at work to come over her if he hadn't volunteered to stay with Willie. How old is Irene? Late twenties I'd guess. That's what, fifteen, sixteen years between her and Jeff. (Alice realized with a start that her sister was fifteen years older than she was.) *What would Evelyn and I be doing if we were together right now?* Alice wondered. *Probably talking about our kids and our houses. Evelyn never had to go to work. We certainly wouldn't be doing math problems together and sewing clothes for handicapped people!* Chuckling to herself, Alice McGowan moved into the kitchen to inspect the contents of her refrigerator.

As it happened, Jeff and Irene were behaving in a fairly unmathmatical manner, with Jeff watching his half-open door with one eye while reading from the somewhat battered and rumpled magazine, as both of them periodically doubled over in fairly juvenile mirth.

Whether intentionally or not, Willie had located a recent issue of Mad magazine which featured 'Longshot'-a takeoff on Mike Longstreet, a blind detective featured on NBC. Companioning him were Chief Ironbutt, obvious parody of the paraplegic policeman played by Raymond Burr, as well as Canyon, easy cognate of Cannon, the overweight private-eye.

"I brought my dog Max." Max for Pax, probably in turn standing for peace?"

"Yes, I know," says the lady of the house, where the investigation is now focusing. "He left little clues all over the rug!"

At a later time, Longshot announces, "It's Chief Ironbutt. I can tell by the way he wheezes and smacks his lips." Later still, Longshot (with dog,) is in hot pursuit of the villains, and running down an alley, he falls over Ironbutt's wheelchair-about the time Canyon becomes lodged in the front door, necessitating a tow-truck and removal of the front of the house.

Irene's favorite part was the scene in which the blind investigator announces "I may not be able to see, but I have four other senses…" and in the next frame he is shown bound, gagged, earmuffed, finger-taped, etc. while his adversaries get on with their Dirty Work. "Tell me the truth?" Irene was holding her sides. "Did you ask him to give us this one?"

"No," Jeff said, actually wishing, rather, that he could take the credit. "I didn't even look at it until just now!"

"Whatever happened about the dirty trick we pulled on Willie?" Irene asked. Neither of them had much felt like discussing the events of That Evening, since there is sometimes the danger of over-discussing things. "I mean, was Willie mad?" Irene prompted. "Angry, I mean?"

Still, Jeff hesitated until the silence got too long for comfort, and he asked, "Irene, I can talk to you about stuff-can't I?"

"Without any hint of a quip," Irene said quietly. "It would be hard for two people to share much more than we have in what-? the three weeks we've known each other, wouldn't it-Jen?"

Jen took a deep breath and told.

"Oh-" Irene said when her friend had done. "Wasn't that scary? Or did it just make you mad?"

"Some of both, I guess," Jennifer told her. "Made me-well-wonder too, I suppose."

Irene nodded slightly. "Stuff like that happened in the girl's cottage down at School," she said a moment later, sounding as if she were very far away. "My friend Charlie said it happened in the boys', too. It's natural enough to wonder."

"But I guess the thing that really got me" Jeff/Jen complained, "was not knowing what Ms. Larson heard, then having her talk to me like that, not knowing what she was really thinking,, then she just handed me back the panties that Willie'd taken out of my locker basket and she never mentioned it again, just like it wasn't any big deal or something."

"Is it?" Irene asked.

"I-don't-know," Jen/Jeff admitted hesitantly. "It's just not <u>knowing</u>."

"But at least she didn't call the Police or turn you over to the Principal," Irene offered helpfully. "Do you think Willie'll leave you alone after this?"

"I imagine-if I don't give him any reason to bug me--?" Jeff wasn't sure whether this was really no or not.

"What are you gloomy gusses doing up here?" Lorna demanded, stepping into the room. "Naughty, naughty." She shook a finger at Jeff when she spied the magazine, still hanging from his left hand. "You guys ready for lunch, or do you have some more 'Math' to finish?"

"Tell Mom just a couple more polynomials, Sis, and we'll be down!"

"Have you ever thought about getting a dog?" Alice McGowan inquired, when they were all sat down to the table. She looked horrified at Irene who appeared to be choking on her tuna salad until she realized that the blind woman was laughing. "I'm sorry. Did I say something wrong?"

"I just thought of a funny story," Irene said through her napkin. Recovering from the coughing fit, she quickly reviewed her list of responses to this irritatingly prevalent query. (*Yes, at age 27, I likely would have thought of such an obvious possibility. Yes.*) But the real question was always "why don't you have a dog?" "The easy answer," she said finally, "Is it's cheaper to feed a cane." She fished her four-foot aluminum specimen with it's black rubber golf-grip from under the table. "Matilda and I can go pretty much anywhere a dog can."

Looks like a shepherd's crook, Alice noted inwardly, eyeing the hooked top of the formidable-looking silver cane. "I'd think a dog would be protection though," she said aloud.

"Maybe," Irene said noncommittally. "A lot of people think so, but if a dog is looking out for muggers, he or she isn't going to be doing a very good job of watching the terrain right in front of you."

Alice bit her sandwich without comment.

"You know though," Irene interjected somewhat placatingly into the ensuing silence. "I think the thing that would bug me the most is having to spend a month at a training center to learn how to walk with the dog and the like, and that'd be too much like being in boarding school again-I just wouldn't do it."

"Lorna," Jeff interjected, in order to break what looked like a new round of argument. "Do you think somebody could build something that would fit in your pocket that could talk, like say numbers or something?"

"Nearly anything's theoretically possible," his sister said, almost on reflex. "Why though?"

"Like a little computer to do math problems," Jeff explained.

Lorna thought about it. "I suppose you could run ten or twelve little tape loops each with a number recorded on it," she mused, "or, maybe somebody could make a device like a slide rule but with the numbers recorded on some kind of tape or record." The idea was intriguing. "I guess I always thought that once blind people could read Braille, their problems were pretty much solved."

"I guess that's only about half the story."

"If that much," Irene agreed.

Lorna watched Irene make her way from the dining room table back to the living room. She swept the cane in arcs in front of her, turning when her cane tip encountered a chair, slowing to a stop when the cane rebounded back from something directly in front of her.

"A robot might do something like that," she mused. "And you wouldn't have to use huge TV cameras or sophisticated computers either." She filed away the notion for further consideration later. A lot could come from people thinking about old problems in new ways, or-as Irene had pointed out, just leaving well enough alone sometimes and sticking with the solution you've got!

Chapter 11.

Alternatives!!

Willie proved, all in all, an able enough assistant to Lorna, making up in dogged persistence whatever he might lack in insight. Indeed, Willie put in so many more hours than requested, that Irene and Jennifer strongly suspected that he'd developed rather a crush on Jeff's vigorous, take-charge sister.

With Elizabeth Larson's help, some early issues of 'The Mother Earth News', and 'Blaire and Kechem's Country Journal' were procured. After some initial confabulation with Lorna, the Seamstresses were hard at work with novel materials and a few-less-than-utilitarian designs, to supplement Irene's serious work already under way.

Chancing to glance at a brochure from Radio Shack, Jeff was struck with an inspiration. Some conversations with the proprietor of the local Radio Shack, who happened to be a HAM operator, an inspired tinkerer and a neighbor, coupled with Jeff's own facility for doing things with his hands, took the project in still another direction-and work on the Birthday Dress continued apace.

Jeff's fairly petulant foray into the Home Economics Department at school-domain and cherished principality of Alma Jensen, turned out to be a god-send to the overall project, in spite of the upswelling of guilt it had caused at the time. Irene and Gussie were so busy turning out garments for school (both Jeff and Lorna's junior high, and the admissions committee at the technical college), that the dress for Lorna would have languished entirely had it not been for Miss Jensen's gathering enthusiasm.

Herself an older sister of many brothers, for whom she'd cooked, sewed, and any number of other things, Miss Jensen was charmed, though bemused by the sweetness of character which must underlie a boy's resolve to make a dress for his older sister. Through this apprehension of hers may have been somewhat of an idealization, the real effort that Jeff had obviously poured into the enterprise was obvious when two days after their first interview, he returned with a list containing answers to most of the questions she'd asked.

In due course, Miss Jensen met Irene at the latter's home, and like everyone else, Miss Jensen was impressed by the array of adaptive and adaptable garments Irene was preparing for display.

"Can we all fit into a Volkswagen Bug?" she inquired. "I thought we should choose the material today, if our birthday is so near…"

They drove to Arland's Fabric and Sewing Supply in the older and Richer part of town, there to pick out by sight-and touch-yardage in a sunny-yellow, cotton and acetate blend and the other things necessary for the construction of even a simple dress such as was proposed.

Miss Jensen sniffed somewhat when Jeff broached the part of the dress-making effort that made it uniquely Lorna-but did what she could do to make even that--! as tasteful and decorous as possible.

"Please! Don't tell Lorna," Jeff implored the advanced (or back-logged) sewing students with whom he shared the Fifth Period independent work time. "It's supposed to be a surprise."

While the girls variously observed that Lorna would now truly look like the woman from outer space, or perhaps be snapped up by the electric utility-the secret was kept.

"Yes, dear?" Miss Jensen peered up from her desk as Jeff, with the dress finally completed, folded and wrapped, stood in front of her.

"Um. Irene and I would like to invite you to the party we're having for Lorna," Jeff said.

Alma Jensen grew slightly pink, smiling back at the student. "Dear me. That would hardly be proper," she said, in a voice so low as to be nearly a whisper. Then, perceiving that Jeffrey's feeling were hurt, she relented sufficiently to say, "the offer is very kind, you know, but it is not correct-for teachers to attend the social events of their students. But please enjoy yourselves in my stead." She removed her glasses, giving them a vigorous polishing with a lace-edged hanky. "Being able to assist in such a project as yours is all the thanks one could need."

As Jeff was walking out of the Home-Ec complex, for the last time--? Possibly not… Miss Jensen called after him, "Extend my best Birthday wishes to your sister."

The day of the Exhibition was cool and crisp. Most evidence of last month's Inadvertent Arsony was covered now with new paint. A section of public lawn, across the street from the library, where the exhibition was centered, had been roped and barricaded as newly planted grass sprouted in the April damp.

The library grounds, painstakingly groomed and manicured by the Yard-

work team, was thronged with students, teachers, parents, and local officials.
Inside the library, a table, well-draped with oil-cloth, and it's similarly
protected surroundings, was buzzing with preschool brothers and sisters,
recipients of Operation Kid Care, all eager to display play-doughed, finger-
painted and crayoned masterpieces. Posters, banners and early garlands
festooned the library inside and out, and evidence of other efforts in the month-
long program were everywhere.

When their time came, Jeff, Irene, Lorna and Willie huddled (for
dramatic purposes), behind the large, plastic tarp which was stretched tightly
between two front pillars of the library porch. The tarp was painted in huge,
white letters "COMMUNITY SERVICE MONTH!"

"If you had to come up with a name for this veritable conglomeration of
projects," Ms. Larson began, "you would call it, simply, Alternatives." She
strode down the broad library steps to the immaculate lawn below.

Along one side of the steps, next to the railing, a ramp had been laid.
Built by Lorna, with the help of Mr. Verbaun, the high school shop teacher, the
ramp had lengths of angle iron fitted to it's bottom side, running width-wise.
These allowed the ramp to lock securely into the steps, but made the unit (also
provided with low, wooden guards on each side), to be picked up and moved.

"We will be seeing the work, and the co-operation of three individuals,
each of whom has managed to step out of his or her own situation and set of
problems, in order to help someone else." On cue, Willie Jackson emerged
from behind the banner-sign and slipped into the library. He emerged
presently, with a wheelchair.

"First," Ms. Larson continued, "we have a guest to our school program,
Irene Carrol, a woman without sight who is not only a designer of clothing for
the handicapped, but as we will see, a seamstress and a sewing teacher in her
own right. Irene will be attending a technical college this Fall, to further her
career in clothes-design with a difference, an alternative."

Irene squirmed uncomfortably in her temporary hide-away.

"We aren't showing you the people yet," Ms. Larson went on, "because
we feel the visual effects will be striking, but felt that some explanation might
be in order first." There were a few giggles, somewhat nervous ones, from the
crowd assembled in front of the library.

"In a sense," Ms. Larson proceeded to the next item of the agenda, "the
person who made all of this..." She waved her hand inclusively. ..."At least
'combinable' is one of our own seventh-graders, a first time participant, who

volunteered to assist and even teach Irene, who lacked people to read study materials for her. In the process, Jeff learned a good bit himself, I fancy."

"Jeff's sister, Lorna, who is one of our ninth-graders, is designer of this alternative rampway to allow wheelchair-bound persons to enter and exit our library with safety and ease. And," Ms. Larson smiled, "it uses no electricity or petroleum fuel!"

With this, Willie rolled the wheelchair to the base of the ramp, guiding it's front wheels between the side runners provided, in order to assure a safe and orderly ascent.

"Lorna and her wheelchair ramp project," said Ms. Larson (Lorna stepped out from behind the banner, but before people could comment, the teacher continued) "will be ably assisted by another seventh-grader, young Willard Jackson who will serve as pilot!" Willie took his seat in the wheelchair.

"AS she said" Lorna told the crowd, "this is about alternatives." The crowd laughed genuinely. "Alternatives have to do with doing different things, or the same things in different ways. This coat I'm wearing, for instance, is made out of newspaper." The crowd laughed again. "It's very warm," Lorna told them. "It's virtually free. It does tend to get a little wet, but a spray of Scotch-guard will take you through a rainstorm." Lorna paused for effect, turning to show the ankle-length garment of laminated newspaper. "I'm not suggesting that we wear newspaper clothes, though it would be cheaper-just to point out how there are always more ways than one to do something." She strode up the stairs, took a pair of ropes which lay coiled on the broad library porch, and tossed them down to Willie.

Willie caught the ropes and pulled. The wheelchair rolled backward, smoothly ascending the ram with a sound not unlike a fishing wheel being wound.

"A device called a ratchet," said Lorna, "prevents the chair from rolling back down. When you want to come down," Willie pulled another rope and did-"a thing called a governor makes sure that you do so slowly."

"These ropes are safe up to a full ton," Lorna declared. "And these pulleys up there," she pointed to a double-wheeled mechanism hanging from a stout porch rafter, "provide what we call a Technical Advantage. That one," Lorna pointed at the larger of the wheels, "carries the rope Willie actually pulled. You may have noticed that Willie was pulling a lot of line in order to go a fairly short way. That's because the wheel is big. This wheel though, this pulley-" she pointed next to the smaller of the set, "-turns just a little way compared to the amount of pulling you do. This way, a little bit of power, over a bit more time, can do a whole lot of work-and anybody can do it." Lorna took the reins from Willie, and after re-checking the two hooks which secured the lines from the smaller pulley to the chair's rear wheel, she handed the ropes to a child of four or five who had come up to inspect. The crowd applauded as the chair, once more, mounted the stairs.

"Thank you, Lorna. As some of you doubtless know," Ms. Larson said indulgently, "our Lorna has her heart set on becoming a woman engineer."

"It may come as somewhat of a surprise to you," Jeff called to the audience, "that I'm wearing a skirt."

"You're wearing a skirt!" Irene feigned surprise. "You found the wrong clothes, I'm supposed to be the blind person!" (Laughter, somewhat uncomfortable, from the crowd of watchers.)

"Sorry Irene," Jeff said. "I'll change." Jeff wore a long skirt-like garment of blue denim, with zippers running in front and back running from hem nearly to crotch. He stepped back behind the banner-tarp and re-emerged in somewhat odd-looking but very serviceable trousers, which obviously were one and the same garment as the skirt.

Irene stepped behind the banner next, and whereas she had been wearing the trousers (the same design as Jeff's), she now wore a skirt. "Two-way zippers," Irene explained, displaying the seam. "Like when you zip sleeping bags together. If you zip the panels front and back, you've got a skirt. Zip them at the inseams, you create pants. These folds, which are secured on the inside of the legs by four snaps, allow you to fold in some of the extra cloth that you might want in a skirt, but not in a pair of jeans."

Jeff demonstrated the hidden snaps at ankle and knee and the pleat-like folds which could be used to tuck unwanted material almost completely out of sight.

Alice McGowan clamped on her best troublesome client grin, as other office workers about her tittered at the "Cute" antics of her son. After all, a year ago you'd never get the kid up in front of any public group, let alone half the town... Put it all in perspective and it all turns out to be in good fun. *I never suspected to raise a daughter who'd build a trolley up the library steps either!*

She consulted her watch. Lunchtime was nearly over and it was time to get back to the office. She waved at Lorna and Jeff, then started to wave at Irene, caught herself and called "great project, kids. Fine work, Irene-" She even bestowed a benevolently mother-like smile upon Willie Jackson who was just then wriggling uncomfortably as if not sure whether he was to be included in the general accolade. As she was slithering through the crowd toward the parking lot, Mr. Osborne the Principal intercepted her, shaking her hand with a damp but earnest grip.

"Two very bright kids," he said. "We feel very fortunate to have them."

Alice smiled her thanks. *That was certainly better than a visit from the fire department or the police.* Still she marveled at how nervous a person, child or parent, could get when you saw a principal bearing down on you!

She turned again, continued toward her car. *I think you'd be around, James.* She could almost feel her tall, rather irreverent husband-so much like Lorna-walking beside her, watching with her. *We all must have done something right.* She turned her head once more before turning into the parking lot around the corner of the gymnasium building. Behind her, the doings continued.

"Some people in wheelchairs" Irene was saying, "have no particular difficulty getting dressed and undressed. For some, it is torture. For many folks, a trip to the restroom can take several times as long as for me or you. This design," she brushed the skirt-garment she wore, "is not only handy if you have trouble making up your mind what to wear, or if like Jeff you can't find your own clothes." She grinned over at Jeff. "But with properly-designed garments underneath, it can provide many more alternatives in dressing, undressing, and caring for oneself."

"To conclude this contribution," Ms. Larson intervened, laughing. "There is, I believe, the matter of a birthday present, a Presentation by Jeff to his Sister, which is, incidentally a debut of Jeff's own sewing skill and-appreciation for alternatives."

"What my mother and little brother won't do to get me into a dress!" Lorna said ruefully. She shucked out of the newspaper coat which, lined with sack paper, had left the garment underneath free of newsprint. "Solar energy dress," Lorna announced.

But before anybody could comment further on what Lorna wore, some disturbance down near the end of the block drew attention that way. A loud "Wait for Me!" issued from Mr. Malcolm, resident of the nearby retirement home, who had just bumped his own wheelchair up over the curbing and was careering along the sidewalk to Lorna's ramp.

"I heard all the commotion, so I came over," Mr. Malcolm announced. "Damned tired of sitting at the bottom of these steps while somebody hands books down to me." He made something between a smile and a leer. "Librarians won't bring me what I really want to read anyway."

Willie helped Mr. Malcolm line up with the ramp and hitched the elderly man's chair to Lorna's contraption.

"Going up!" Mr. Malcolm called, hauling in rope like a fisherman with too much play in his line. At the top of the steps he paused before turning, grinned broadly at Lorna. "What would a pretty girl like you recommend as a good read to while away a Saturday afternoon?" Mr. Malcolm asked with a chortle. "One of them love stories, mebbe?"

"Oh, I'd say Elementary Physics by Weidner and Sells would be about right," Lorna answered, without cracking a smile.

"Honestly, Jeff," their mother exclaimed, when Lorna first wore the dress with it's unconventional adornments along the sleeve and across the front of it. "I hoped you'd help me civilize your sister somewhat, not help her to look-like a walking electrician's bench!" But crinkles at the corner of her eyes belied Mrs. McGowan's grim facade.

"Velcro, mom," Jeff said reassuringly. "Comes off for washing."

Over at Irene's, two days before the Exhibition in the heart of town, the dress had been presented by two of it's three principal authors. Jeff had stepped into the bathroom, shedding his jeans and sweater in order to serve as a display rack for the sunshine-yellow sheath with the checker-board pattern of solar cells and spider-web tracery of red and black.

"I'm afraid I needed to borrow your new soldering iron, Sis," Jeff admitted. He unplugged a wire from one of the little Radio-Shack solar cells attached to the dress. "Like little electronic Legos," Jeff said self-satisfiedly. "Hook 'em in series or parallel." He showed Lorna the direct current power receptacle at the end of the three-quarter length sleeve, "like a cigarette lighter in a car. Plug in anything you can put in a DC jack," he said.

"I absolutely love it," Lorna smirked. "Mom'll have a fit! And those things aren't cheap Jeff-gosh."

"I got a job reading for Irene," Jeff demurred. "The state pays me for helping her complete her courses."

Lorna fingered the receptacle on Jeff's left elbow. "What should I plug into it I wonder?"

"Alternatives," Jeff told her.

"Well, take off the damned thing and let her see if it fits!" Irene scolded. "Speaking of coursework," she continued, "I can do equations till they come out my ears, thanks to you and Jeff. Though, if I get beyond X, Y, and Z, I'll have to become a foreign coin collector. What I'd like to know is why?"

"Why what?" Lorna asked.

"Why should I care what X and Y are? I never see any in real life."

"Oh," said Lorna absently, "let's say you've got maybe one thousand dollars to go to school next year, and let's say you pay seventy-five dollars for registration fees, and you want to know how much you have left to spend each trimester of school. You'd get the answer from $3x+75=1000$, where X is the amount you can spend each quarter."

Irene made a great show of cogitation. "What do I do with the one third of a penny?"

Chapter 12.

Gifts

After the presentation ceremony Irene, Jeff and Lorna went over to Cunningham's Drug in the shopping center, taking stools at the fountain counter.

"They do this Service Month thing every year?" Irene asked.

"More or less," Lorna told her. "How did you know about it in the first place, Irene?"

"Oh, you know, that little piece of news at the end of the six O'clock program. Still, that's not why Jeff here and I actually met, or wasn't <u>supposed</u> to be..."

"Really?" Jeff asked, taken aback. "What do you mean?"

"Well-it must have been a year ago or so. I wrote a note to the Principal of your school asking for somebody to work with me, go to the store with, look up things in the phone book, find needles I dropped, watch movies-you know."

Jeff's ears got warmer, and Irene continued, saying "I don't know how the ad I wrote ended up in this year's pool of community jobs. There was a girl who came around a couple times last year."

"A girl named Julie?" Jeff cracked up.

Their order arrived as Jeff was laughing, drawing stares from others around the counter, but Jeff ignored them. "Oh, that's great," he said when he finally regained control.

"I see I have a reputation around school," Irene remarked, nipping the end of her straw paper and blowing the straw free. "Oh, I don't want to say anything mean about the girl," Irene said between swigs of her ice cream soda. "Let's just say that she'd probably have been happier if I'd been confined to a hospital bed, didn't know how to talk and maybe wet my pants occasionally. What does she say about me?"

"That you're a pain," Jeff informed her.

"This is news?" Well I mean, she kept grabbing my cane in my hand and saying things like 'if you had a doggy,' and 'you do so well...!' That's partly why I almost choked on my lunch over at your house that time. Gee-I hope I didn't make you mom feel bad."

"I think it pretty much passed over her," Lorna said. "So you in effect got recycled."

"Yeah." Irene wrinkled her nose, staring somewhat ceilingward. "I guess I did!"

"You mean," Jeff said, "my name was almost Julie?"

Irene noisily slurped her straw. "Sorry about that," she told nobody in particular. "When I was a kid my mom wouldn't let me get away with that, so I vowed that when I was gig," Irene patted herself, "I'd do it every chance I got."

"If you children wouldn't mind entertaining one another," Lorna said, slipping off her stool, "I just remembered an errand Mother asked me to do and which I'd forgotten."

"So," Irene inquired without noticeable shifting of conversational gears. "How are things with you and Ms. Larson? You getting along okay?"

"Most of the time," Jeff said. "Except she still confuses me. Sometimes when I really think she understands me, then she'll turn around and make me feel like some kind of convict."

"She thinks very highly of you. And if she seems a little inconsistent at times, I imagine she's just trying to keep you from getting hurt.

"She's not always had things easy herself," Irene added, after another pull at her chocolate soda. "I can't really share her story, because it was a confidence, but let's say that she's had her troubles-griefs, in her time."

Jeff nodded, in spite of Irene. "Ms. Larson told me something interesting the other day," Jeff said, rather dreamily. "She told me that if I was going to be different, I needed to be very good at something-something that hardly anybody else has, that can make me different in a special way. Like if I wanted to sew, then I should be the best student in the home-ec class, or if I wanted to work with," he hesitated, "handicapped people-I should learn Braille and Sign and a lot of other things that most other people don't know how to do."

"I've always found that to be true," Irene agreed. "As a blind person, I've found that if you don't want to stay a child all your life, or some kind of community pet, you've got to stand out somehow, either as an interesting person, or at the very least, as a huge pain." This time, neither of them laughed.

"I'm going to tell you a secret now," she said then, "that's going to sound like I'm coming on you like your mom or something. You're a very impressive person. I think it's wonderful how you can relate with women and girls-and people who are Different, superficially anyhow. Maybe that is enough, enough being different I mean. If it isn't though, remember, you've got time to decide."

"You do sound like an old lady," Jeff grinned.

"Told you so." Irene squeezed her friend's arm. "Just, don't let the Willies of the world shape you into something you're not ready to be."

"I'm back," Lorna announced. She unzipped her purse, rummaging inside for change. The bag which contained her purchase rattled as she did so.

"On me," Irene declared. "I really enjoyed the company, and a chance to get out."

Walking out of the shopping center, toward Irene's street, "You're still a woman, McGowan" came Willie's voice from a block or more away.

"Tell the little snot thank you," Irene remonstrated.

"You just <u>wish</u>, Jackson," Jeff called back and whatever Willie answered then was lost in a swirling gust of wind, leaves, and trash paper.

"Hey Irene?"

"What, Hon?"

"If you had such a bad time," Jeff asked, "with that other girl I mean? How come was it you wanted to meet <u>me</u>?"

"Don't know really," Irene shook her head. "Must've been something about your voice-you sounded as scared as I felt."

Home at last, Jeff took himself up to his room, closed the door and sat down at his desk, propping chin on elbows. Considering. Very Good at Something. Irene and Ms. Larson seemed to be in agreement about that, but good at what? Irene had her sewing, Lorna had her engineering-her "innovation," as she'd call it. Even Willie had his rubbery resilience, his ability to face down all those kids who didn't like him-and they were numerous. "What have I got?" Jeff asked, alone in the silence of the room.

Today Jeff had worn a skirt. Done it right out in public, in front of <u>everybody,</u> even Mom! Had that been, though, rather like being a clown, or as Irene had said, a sort of community pet? Is that what I am? Jeff wondered. *Or am I the only one who feels like this?*

All kinds of guys on TV dressed and acted to one extent or another as girls. Why, look at that Flip Wilson character. But they did it to make people laugh-*why do I?* Thinking back, Jeff guessed that he was seven or eight when he'd first put on Lorna's Sunday dress and scarf. It'd been way too big, and he hadn't been careful then and Mom had caught him, but she'd just scolded Jeff about wrinkling his sister's best dress and sighed in that way that said "just another phase." Like when Jeff had wanted to dye his hair green so he could be a Martian. Except, it hadn't really been a phase, had it?

Not for the first time, Jeff wondered if Mom really didn't know, or if she just didn't want to know. *She'd probably feel guilty since Lorna and I don't have a dad,* he decided. Mom worried about that a lot. Jeff could hardly remember his dad, except as somebody who used to carry him around on his shoulders and who played a ukulele and sang funny songs sometimes. Jeff was pretty sure though, that not having a dad didn't have much to do with how he was. Lots of kids didn't have dads, and so far as Jeff knew-*well, how many people know about me? Irene, Lorna, maybe-Willie!* The last name caused a flush of embarrassment to wash over Jeff. Wouldn't it be nice if there was some place where it didn't matter? Like if everybody was like Irene, but nobody had to lose their eyesight or anything. Was there such a place? Jeff didn't know. There were books though, he supposed and one way or another he figured he'd try to find out. *If such a place doesn't exist, maybe I could make one.* With no idea how, he planted the idea as a seed of a dream and vowed to himself to cherish it. Maybe Irene would have some thoughts on the subject too.

I could write to Dear Abby or one of those people. But, they always sounded like they were scolding kids who had real problems. Then, Jeff got another notion. *I'll write a letter like I'm a mom who's son dresses like a girl and has a lot of friends who are girls, and say I* approve *of this kid, and see what they say then!* Maybe that was Jeff's-Jennifer's thing to be really good at, to find out the <u>why</u> of whatever's wrong with you being a girl-if you want to be-

Lorna ascended the stairs slowly, one stair at a time, just as glad Mom had yet to return from work. *She's putting in overtime, doubtless, after taking time out to watch us today.* She turned into her own room, opening her closet door. *Face it,* she told the rack of school clothes. *You've got a goony brother-any goonier than me, though? Really?* The kid could use some lessons in protecting himself a little better, but, she suspected, his choice of Irene as a pal was one of the smarter things Jeff had ever done. Irene didn't take anything from anyone! She found the right hook and slipped the hanger off the rack.

Lorna rapped twice on Jeff's door and walked in, holding out one of last year's dresses in one hand, her recent purchase in the other. "There." She tossed the K-Mart bag on his bed. "Now you can quit pawing through my drawers. Better not let Mom find them though, or she'll snatch me bald and send you off to boot camp. And <u>here</u>." She held up the blue dress on it's hanger (the same one that weeks ago, their mother had discovered at the bottom of Jeff's closet) "You can keep it. Yuck!" Then, having delivered this rebuke, or perhaps license-she said "and we can talk. Okay?"

Rather too taken aback for words, Jeff merely nodded, a lump forming where he tried to swallow.

"Good," Lorna said, turned and went back downstairs.

Jeff spent several minutes staring out the window. At last he picked up the bag from his bed, looked inside, hid it at the bottom of his winter drawer. The bureau mirror confronted him as he straightened. He made a face at his reflection, pouting his lips and widening his eyes until they strained. "Lots of time ahead of us, Jennifer. Only, what do we do next?"

www.ingramcontent.com/pod-product-compliance
Lightning Source LLC
Chambersburg PA
CBHW031248280526
45784CB00004B/1772